GOOD STORIES REVEAL as much, or more, about a locale as any map or guidebook. Whereabouts Press is dedicated to publishing books that will enlighten a traveler to the soul of a place. By bringing a country's stories to the English-speaking reader, we hope to convey its culture through literature. Books from Whereabouts Press are essential companions for the curious traveler, and for the person who appreciates how fine writing enhances one's experiences in the world.

"Coming newly into Spanish, I lacked two essentials—a childhood in the language, which I could never acquire, and a sense of its literature, which I could."

—Alastair Reid, *Whereabouts: Notes on Being a Foreigner*

S P A I N

A TRAVELER'S LITERARY COMPANION

EDITED BY

PETER BUSH

&

LISA DILLMAN

WHEREABOUTS PRESS
BERKELEY, CALIFORNIA

Published in the United States by
Whereabouts Press
Berkeley, California
www.whereaboutspress.com

Distributed to the trade by
Consortium Book Sales & Distribution

Map of Spain by BookMatters

Manufactured in the United States of America

Library of Congress Cataloging-in-Publication Data

Spain : a traveler's literary companion /
edited by Peter Bush (1946–)
& Lisa Dillman (1967–).
p.   cm.—(Travelers' literary companions)
ISBN 1-883513-12-x (trade paperback : alk. paper)
1. Short stories, Spanish—Translations into English.
2. Spanish fiction—20th century—Translations into English.
3. Spain—Fiction.
I. Bush, Peter R., 1946–
II. Dillman, Lisa 1967–.
III. Traveler's literary companion.
PQ6267 .E8S63   2003
863' .01083246—dc21   2003002251

5 4 3 2 1

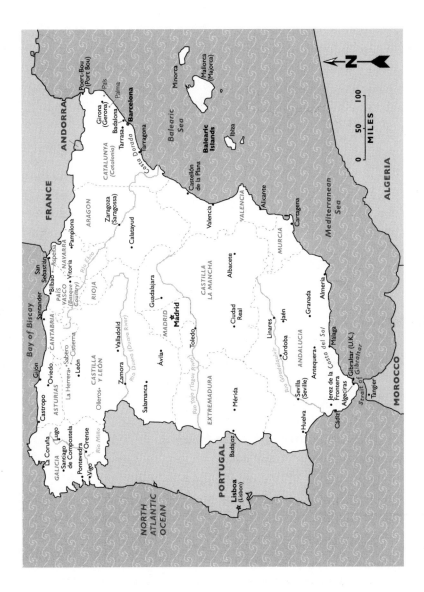

Contents

Preface

SPAIN IS A LAND OF SURPRISES for travelers and readers alike. They may find the donkey and mule a vanishing species in the south; and in the north landscapes are often green and misty, and it can rain for days on end. The countryside has depopulated and Spain has large cities where inhabitants cram into apartment buildings creating some of the largest urban concentrations of humanity in Europe. With an industrialized economy, the country no longer depends on income from migrant workers. Spain imports unskilled workers from West and North Africa to harvest the year-round crops that modern irrigation and plastic greenhouses have brought to the once parched Andalusian landscape, where only seventy years ago a landless peasantry defended the Spanish Republic against the Fascist army of General Franco. By the time television came to villages like Olleros in 1963, the economic changes were beginning that would transform the country and empty out the villages into the Eldorados of Barcelona and Madrid, Frankfurt and Paris.

This collection strives to go beyond commonplaces about the bull's skin that is the shape of Spain to writing that is vibrant with a real Spain whose soul Federico García Lorca already complained in 1918 was "beyond the great caravans of rowdy tourists fond of cabarets and grand hotels" ("Holy Week in Granada"). When Juan Goytisolo relates his narrow escapes from death on a French road and then in a bullrun in Elche de la Sierra (through ironic stream of consciousness celebrating the "determination to fight tooth and nail against oblivion" and the many threads of experience and memory that converge at such intense moments), the reader faces not the Romantic Spain of Bizet's *Carmen* or Hemingway's Pamplona but a first Spanish essay into existential autobiography.

In these pages you will find Miguel Delibes's grizzled peasants hunting with rusty shotguns in the hills of Old Castile. In Xosé Luís Méndez Ferrín's story, Galician artists of the 1920s prowl the melancholy foggy streets of Santiago de Compostela, their encounters with mysterious rings, triangles, and ellipses recounted by a narrator familiar with the Bauhaus, German cinema, and the Battle of Stalingrad. In Nivaria Tejera's story, the young girl narrator remembers her father's disappearance at the beginning of the civil war in the Canary Islands. You will also encounter more familiar urban experiences: Carme Riera recreates the solitude of the lonely old woman in Barcelona; Lucía Extebarria's blasé hip lesbian is into combat boots and Eurostudy and rebels against the heavy velvet and antiques of bourgeois parents in Madrid. The writers selected here reflect a rich Spanish palimpsest of memory, history, and modernity in stories that tell of a complex transition from civil war to dictatorship to democracy.

After General Franco's death in 1976 politicians ushered

in democratic freedoms, regional autonomy, and rights of expression in Basque, Catalan, and Galician. These languages are being fully developed by writers like Bernardo Atxaga, Quim Monzó, and Manuel Rivas—present in this collection—into supple instruments for capturing aspects of contemporary reality. Eschewing folkloric flourishes and narrow provincial horizons, Atxaga recalls the fascists in the classroom; Rivas, the troubled sexuality of the celibate priest as witnessed through the confessional and mocked by uncowed Galician women; and Monzó, the brittle, mundane relationship of a middle-class Catalan couple with their beach and city apartments. New literary languages grapple with a new Spanish modernity.

In the 1980s most politicians favored a form of historical amnesia for the population: forget the past and it will go away; Spaniards are newly democratic, liberal, Europeans and have cast off the phantoms of the bloody fratricide of 1936–39. Many of our stories are about men and women struggling with memory, recovering a past that lingers on in the lives of Spaniards, in intimate memories of hatreds that have to be confronted. Nuria Amat's high-society wedding proceeds alongside conversations about Catalan democrats who have perished in German concentration camps. Dulce Chacón narrates Extremaduran militia-woman Isidora's disturbing re-entry into life as a servant when she returns from the front. The Spanish Civil War lives on in recollection. Rafael Chirbes dwells on the dinginess of the 1940s, the years of hunger, black-marketeering, and grinding poverty, where the men on Madrid's Gran Vía do whatever they can and whatever it takes to get by. Amaia

Gabantxo's grandmother struggles against Alzheimer's, clinging to fleeting reminiscences of bean-picking in the fields or of the bombing of Guernika by Hitler's airplanes.

The panic felt in Laura Freixas's fairy tale of an anarchic island breaking away from the fatherland gently satirizes the fears of those who did not welcome the demise of fascism. Barcelona and Madrid, rival cities and industrial and political capitals respectively, become microcosms of Spain as migrants in the '50s and '60s flow into ramshackle shanty towns where Marsé's artful dodgers, Java and Itchy and their gang, survive on petty theft. The economic prosperity of Europeanization eventually displaces these Andalusians, Galicians, and Murcians into cheap municipal housing, and their chase is on to become middle class and accepted.

An Almodóvar streak zanily hits the streets. Staid Catholic morality is out. Inés Pereira is one of the many bohemian dropouts selling pirated cassettes by the Puerta del Sol, and in Agustín Cerezales's story this punk with a nun's complexion falls for a married accountant. José Ferrer Bermejo's anonymous hero gets lost in the maze of the Madrid metro system and loses his mind while searching for an exit. Javier Puebla evokes in a single page a new cosmopolitan Spain as Koreans, Russians, Moroccans, and others hover around Lavapiés payphones. Grandma's girls in Angela Vallvey's piece think of sex and food: once good girls had to be back home by ten when the night watchman locked the door to the block; now they come and go talking of fellatio.

And the light, beaches, sherry, and a Spanish tempo of life remain. Rosa Chacel captures the luminosity of the siesta and the aroma of spices during the heat of a summer afternoon, with shouting and cats leaping around the patio and a warm intensity of light permeating every dusty corner of mind and body. Sevillian real-estate agents relish their daily round of sherries in the story by Fernando Quiñones, whose narrator amuses himself at the expense of the English. Families play happily on Asturian beaches and the rows of sun-tanning flesh stretch out in San Sebastian in two scenarios of sand with a twist by Julián Ayesta and Javier Marías.

Spain may have modernized out of rural poverty, and may now possess a buoyant tourist industry, a burgeoning bourgeoisie, and champion soccer teams. Nevertheless, like all European countries, it retains differences, its Gaudís and Almodóvars, and a unique historical and literary experience. As Lorca wrote, the magnificent palace of the Alhambra, home to the last Arab monarchs of Spain, "is not and will never be Christian."

Peter Bush

Daydream Island
Laura Freixas

RESTING SERENELY, right there where destiny had put her, she wasn't happy but neither was she sad. It had been a long time since geographers had proclaimed once and for all just where everything belonged; the world was caught in webs of highways and road signs, and good people slept peacefully. The sun and the moon, alternately, traced leisurely circles around it; day followed night and then came dawn; at noon all the church bells struck twelve in unison. Everything was in its place. But at times, looking at herself in the water, she worried that her image was fading. In those moments, she repeated her name uneasily in a loud voice, and her name rang empty, a hollow shell; she couldn't see her reflection in the water, only the gentle rocking of the nets of light upon the waves.

LAURA FREIXAS *(Barcelona, 1958–) is a regular contributor to several newspapers and cultural publications and has translated the diaries of Virginia Woolf and André Gide. She has published two novels, the essay* Mujeres y literatura *(2000), edited the anthology* Madres e hijas *(Anagrama, 1996), and published two books of short stories. "Daydream Island" is taken from the collection* El asesino de la muñeca *(1998).*

One night, however, something unexpected happened: she saw the moon cry. Was it lovesick? It was flushed, and down its smooth, shining cheeks rolled tears of light that slid into the sea with a sigh. Without thinking, she lurched forward to get closer to the moon.

But many centuries of immobility and inactivity had elapsed; barely noticeable bonds imprisoned her and filled her with the taste of rust. She pulled harder, desperately impatient, her gaze fixed upon the distant moon—she hadn't known that she was so solidly anchored, such a captive—until, surprising herself, she suddenly pulled up her rocky roots. When she realized what had happened, she found herself adrift, floating freely. The wind ruffled her green hair, and her stone cheeks burned with excitement.

In the depths of the sea, algae combed their hair with pearly combs. Snails dreamed spiral dreams, oysters soothed their tiny pearls with lullabies, seahorses slept in their stables, and hammerheads took a rest from a hard day's carpentry work. None of them noticed the immense shadow that silently passed above them, carrying on its back streets and streetlights, sleeping inhabitants and their dreams, deserted plazas with murmuring fountains, and stealthy cats dancing on rooftops.

Lost in delight in the darkness, shy and excited, she forgot about the moon, now hidden behind drapes of clouds. Chance had suddenly put the entire world within her reach—other seas and coastlines, all the wonders she had ever dreamed of.

She would go see the Côte d´Azur, with its beaches of fine blue sand and its blue men and Bluebeard, the king, in his blue palace with his blue servants. She would visit the

Costa Dorada; she would see golden sand, silver rocks, and emerald pine trees. And the Costa del Sol, where the sun goes to bed every night hugging a pillow of purple clouds, at the same time that the moon, accompanied by its royal court of stars, pulls up anchor to serenely sail the sky. She would know other seas! The Red Sea, beneath a heavenly vault, red by day and white by night, with black foamy crests on red waves, and blue crabs, and white mussels. The Black Sea . . . it would be exotic and wild. She had heard of its Golden Horn. A black and haughty sea, finished off with a twisted golden shaft, just like a unicorn.

And the Dead Sea? It would be cold and still, poor thing, buried beneath a marble tombstone—an immense tombstone, big enough to cover an entire dead sea, with its motionless waves, open-mouthed whales, and pale mermaid skeletons. On the giant headstone, an inscription, Here lies the Dead Sea. RIP.

The sun began to rise, and she didn't know where she was. News of the disappearance of the isle of Minorca, which had become known that same night, dropped like a bombshell on the Iberian peninsula. Sweating and half crazy, navy commanders fell all over each other giving contradictory orders, while sirens searching for lost ships echoed in the fog, like mourners.

The archbishop of Spain—who had been dragged out of bed by sorrowful acolytes—while still in his slippers, drafted a virtuous speech in which he blamed godless communism for perverting natural law. The council of ministers, meeting with a sense of urgency (under their wrinkled jackets the lapels of fancy pajamas could be seen, and in the confusion nobody noticed the Russian spy under the rug), drafted one calming communiqué after another, which served only to intensify the sense of alarm in the general population. Amid the pandemonium of cries, phone calls, and faxes, frenzied reporters mixed up the Catalogue of Subject Matter and the Index of Expressions, attempting to compose, in time for the morning edition, grim, long-winded editorials that said absolutely nothing. But in the back of everyone's minds lingered the same fear: everything that up until now had been fixed and immovable—monuments and mountain ranges, tombs, traffic lights—could at any moment, with unimagined treachery, begin to move.

The police were given orders to cordon off plazas and parks all over Spain, for fear that the marble statues of Venus and the bronze statues of Mars, empowered by the pernicious example of the island—if they got wind of what was going on—would calmly get down off their pedestals to go pet a stray cat, hunt for mushrooms, play hide-and-seek, or even worse, fool around together under the trees. To increase security, the hooves of horses in equestrian statues were shackled. In Barcelona, a squad of sharpshooters timidly aimed their machine guns at a statue of Columbus, with orders to open fire if they saw him slide down his column like a mischievous child. In Madrid, an entire armored division guarded the majestic Cibeles fountain; and in Gerona, the terrified army dug trenches in front of the cathedral, which could cause a catastrophe if it began to walk down its huge staircase and wander around.

In response to such preparations, panic spread quickly among the upright citizenry. Even the bravest hurried to shut their doors and windows tightly, fearful of witnessing the hair-raising spectacle of streets invaded by triumphal arches, ornamental fountains, and newsstands, slithering and stumbling in frightful chaos. Families chained their pianos to the dining room wall; delighted children immediately suggested building them huts and setting them up to guard their homes, imagining that if anything strange came up the instruments would sound an alarm by feverishly breaking into the Fifth Symphony.

For their part, conscientious priests double-locked the church doors to prevent the rows of pews from escaping at a gallop, followed by altars, kneelers, sacred images, and holy-water fonts leaping along behind. And when people began to regard with suspicion even the candelabras, mirrored wardrobes, and bathtubs in the very homes where they took refuge, symptoms of collective hysteria broke out.

By noon, feeling that it was on the brink of a disaster—since it was obvious that in the worst-case scenario neither the belfries that had decided to go out and see the world nor the Louis XV chairs skipping through the streets were going to respect any kind of curfew—the government decided to settle things once and for all and ordered fifteen warships to retrieve the mutinous island.

Meanwhile, Minorca was excited beyond belief: approaching the beach at Pals, she had just glimpsed the enormous antenna of Radio Liberty, sparkling in the morning sun, and was convinced it was the Golden Horn. She didn't have time to realize her mistake. From one of the warships in pursuit, a lion tamer, hired for the occasion by the government, threw a gigantic net over her, demonstrating his impeccable aim. The whole country, entrenched behind closed doors and windows, between sofas and chests of drawers tied down with rope, followed the details of the capture on television. Minorca let herself be led meekly to the docks in Palma where, amid the cheers of relieved inhabitants, she was met by a band playing military music. Later, she was decorated from head to toe and, in an atmosphere of euphoria, returned with utmost solemnity to her original spot.

One could say that everything is back to normal, no matter how many people go to take a bath and think they see a scornful look on the bathtub, no matter how many cannot avoid an instant of dreadful apprehension when they open the shutters every morning fearing they will see a sidewalk bench clambering up a streetlight. (Although the incident did not make it into the newspapers, everyone knows that two weeks after these events, customs officials in Port-Bou intercepted a coffee table that was attempting to cross the French border disguised as an archbishop.) Heartbroken by the failure of her innocent adventure, Minorca carried on without understanding what had happened, and at times wondered forlornly who was going to take flowers to the Dead Sea.

Translated by Barbara Paschke

The Wedding
Nuria Amat

THE WEDDING INVITATION wasn't written in the family's language. It was written in the language of the State. The wedding presents being delivered to the house on the longest street in the city made it difficult to get in and around once inside. Unavoidable duties were added to the list of thank-you cards to send for the pile of presents received. Last-minute nerves were added to all this helter-skelter. You are too thin, Nena, the ladies said. Don't wear yourself out too soon.

We wanted to leave the country. Have a honeymoon in France, said Nena.

Three men drew up in a car bearing the bridal gown on arms wrapped in sheets of white fabric. They moved it from

NURIA AMAT *(1950–) was born in Barcelona and has lived in Colombia, Mexico, Berlin, Paris, and the United States. She is a novelist, essayist, and short story writer. Her novels,* La intimidad *(1997),* El paisaje del alma *(1999), and* Reina de América *(2003, City of Barcelona Prize for Literature) have established her as a leading writer in the Spanish language. This extract from the 1999 novel charts a tragic love in a Catalonia ravaged by the aftermath of civil war and a dictatorship intent on repressing Catalan culture.*

side to side like a weary, phantom dancer. The dress was secret. Everything else could be seen and admired but not the white bridal dress. The exhibition of presents, like the bride's trousseau, was open to all visitors. Friends and relatives who enjoyed long periods of free time in the afternoon to devote to visiting paraded through the house on the longest street in the city. They said to each other: Let's take a stroll round the exhibition of Nena Rocamora's wedding presents.

Baltus wasn't ashamed to confess that his own hands were responsible for the exhibition of the bride's presents. This form of art is bogus, he would say in his head when congratulated on his decorative talent and good taste. The furniture in the dining room and sitting room shamelessly spat embroidered table linen, sets of gold-edged bone china, canteens of silver cutlery, lamps, cut-glass, and an array of bric-a-brac for the home. A white visiting card with the name of the person who'd sent the present beamed out from the center of each offering. The guests wanted to compare other presents with theirs. There was a lot to consider in this exhibition of bridal presents. The women entered the wedding suite to take a close look at what would clothe Nena's nakedness. The betrothed's intimate garments were laid out on the twin bedspreads. The silk of nightdresses and petticoats slithered over quilts. Whenever an overcurious visitor dared to touch one of the intimate garments on the bed, the display was disfigured and Nena had to rush to repair it. The men didn't usually enter this dark feminine zone. The single aunts said: Too much black silk for my liking. But they stood with mouths wide open expressing their admiration for the bride's trousseau. A little later, a family acquaintance started asking everyone: Where's my present. It must have got lost, she said as she ran from one end of the floor to the other. Her protests got higher pitched, and Nena had to intervene and find a solution: It'll turn up. You'll soon see. Let's look for it.

Anyone would think the woman had lost one of her children in the center of the Plaza de Cataluña, said one of the aunts.

The family acquaintance was gasping and her pulse racing, such was her dismay. All the visitors there at the time started looking for the missing present. They might have been playing at that guessing game—cold, hot, or frozen. Finally, someone found it, and said: Here's the lost present we've been looking for. And faking a happy smile held up a small pink and very twisted jug. The family acquaintance said: Oh, that's a relief. Calmed down, she could now bid farewell to the other visitors.

Aunt Flora didn't stop talking the whole afternoon, said Nena. My nephews and nieces wouldn't leave her skirts. Aunt Flora has a parrot that talks like her, and four parakeets, and two goldfinches. She's funny. And she knows how to talk to children.

The women's perfume left a trail of false expectations in the new house. Nena had fun for a while trying to guess which coat went with which visitor according to the scent they gave off. She organized a mental competition. You've won, Lola, she said. Your perfume's the best of the lot.

When the last of her sisters went, Baltus said: It's time we went too. But they didn't.

Nena thought, I've everything now. But she said: It's cold.

Baltus put his hand on the radiators. They're hot, he said.

It was the cold from the new house. Then Baltus embraced Nena in very solemn fashion. She said: I've lost my shoe. Though she meant there were only four days to the wedding.

Nena sat on the end of the bed, between her black nightdress and white petticoat. She knew about men's bodies thanks to her sisters' blurred silences. However, she didn't know Baltus's body. Sisters never told you the real truth. No one tells you anything here. You have to find out by guesswork. Bodies were boxes of tricks that sprang open to reveal themselves. Men's bodies were like live pillows. You slept with them and afterward had to invent them.

As there were no empty seats, Baltus sat cross-legged on the floor. Like a fakir, he said. His chin was split in two halves that his fingers playfully tried to join up.

The record player was also a wedding present. It had an automatic pickup and let you load six thirty-three RPM records at a time. The music surged again and again as if by magic.

Nena disappeared for a second. She soon returned naked beneath her black nightdress. The living room was almost in darkness. Only a circle of light lit the carpet.

You're so beautiful, Baltus said. Baltus could lead a woman into the center of the dance floor and ensure she was admired by everyone like a star. It sufficed to know how to look at a woman to make her the one most desired of all. It sufficed to know how to look at her and desire her. To love a lot.

As they danced in the center of the floor the windowpanes trembled. Nena's waist trembled. Everything was so new. The kisses didn't finish like full stops. They were long sentences. Endless. Sentences drowning in mouth and belly. That went up and down. Her body grew, her breasts wanted to flee the stage. They bloomed like sickly leaves, swollen on love. Empty for adventure.

Captive in Baltus's arms, Nena felt her body was divided. In front, it was opening. It shut and stretched like a book. The top part reared up, the lower part bucked and stretched. A pleasure that's scary, she said. He said, I love you, to stem her wildness. You had to say I love you whenever love gave a reason to die or commit suicide. I love you was a grip on a reason to live. They were knotted together in the center of the floor. They could stay here but the music said no more. And went silent.

Baltus premiered the sentence. Let's go to bed.

Nena was swathed by love, moved on the mattress as if turning pages or trying to take the veils from her cage. She wanted to breathe. Her body had its own desires. She desired Baltus's body. It was another new desire. Her body snaked, entangled Baltus. You see, she said. And he moaned: What a victory.

Baltus could see his love was life or death. For the rest of time, he said.

But she said: No, I think I'm dying.

Love was long and short. Death less than verse length. Then, she preferred to curl up and let her white skin of a woman possessed slowly cool down.

Afterward she looked at herself naked. It was another invitation to a kiss.

I'm not as thin as they say, she said.

She lit the bedside lamp.

Thin how, said Balthus.

With an imaginary tape he began measuring her body. She eluded centimeters. Or the span of his hands. Then Baltus collapsed on the pillow. He played sudden death. An intangible corpse. He raised his eyelids and showed the whites of his eyes, deader than the dead.

Donkeys gawp, fools get angry, sang Nena trying to be cheerful. They were happy. They held on to the moment.

The next morning, when Baltus got off the tram and started walking in the direction of the bar on the plaza in La Nava, those who passed by him stopped for a second to stare at his solemn face. Baltus was getting married on Saturday, and his face had a Monday or Sunday look to it.

His overcoat collar was pulled up over his ears. It was drizzling. The sky was unpicking the clouds of this leaden winter.

Baltus went into the café and hung his coat on the hanger. A solitary table-football game stretched out its grimy, rusty arms at the back of the room. Four old men were playing cards at the first table. Two wore berets and a third was biting a toothpick. By this time all the café's customers were hungry and fooling their hunger with a glass of water or beer. The choice of what they could lift to their lips depended on the feel of their pockets, the mood of their poverty. In the café on the plaza in La Nava everything that happened in the neighborhood was common knowledge but nobody said a word. Things got out with no need to talk about them. A look was an unfinished story. Centimo coins ran along the floor and disappeared under tables that nobody cleaned. The bulbs were too high up. They dispensed a milky-coffee light. The sombre-colored bar.

Baltus's friends exchanged laughs. The café politics was of the domestic sort. Slipper and dressing-gown politics. And ash in the stove. The other politics was banned. Besides, the walls of this little country had ears rather than windows. The younger parishioners stood by the bar. They were eating Spanish olives. They wanted to laugh at Baltus, who was getting married tomorrow, but nobody dared, Baltus's face called for serious laughs.

His friends said: Baltus, another round on you. The men drank and emptied from their glass all their hunger for words. What will we talk about when we can speak, they asked the glass of words. Habit was stronger than politics.

It was raining hard. At the table next to his, Baltus spotted Ramón. Adam Mestres's friend.

How are you, Ramón, asked Baltus. He was pleased and surprised by this encounter. As children they'd played together in the plaza. He'd lost touch with him since. They patted each other on the back. Ramón said: Come and sit next to me by the stove. His mouth didn't say that. It was the pain in his eyes.

How've you been, asked Baltus.

Ramón kept leaning his head into the heat of the stove. The floor stank of live and dead cigarette butts.

I still can't believe it, said Ramón. It's been horrible. I don't know where to begin. My memory is going. I'm ill. You can't see me.

But rather than revealing his body huddled round the stove, Ramón showed him his hands. His fingers and arms were shaking. I can't keep them still, he said.

And straightaway: They killed Adam in Mathausen, he said.

Are you sure? asked Baltus. I can't believe it.

He began to bite his knuckles.

Murderers, he thought. Criminals, he said. A gang of criminals and murderers.

Pain was a barrier between them and the stove.

How do you know, he asked finally.

Ramón said he knew because he was there. With Adam. We were deported to Germany. I didn't see them kill him but I know it was the SS and I also know how they killed him.

It's not possible, said Baltus.

He raised his hand. Called the waiter and ordered two shots of gin.

Ramón said: When the Americans finally arrived and liberated us I went back to France. First I was in the Hotel Lutetia in Paris and then they put me in an American hospital. Now I go under a false name.

Balthus didn't ask why the false name. It sounded like an American dream.

I'm ill, Ramón said.

They went silent for a while. They drank gin straight, no ice. The gin burned their throats but that was fine. At least, it was more bearable than the sadness.

Smoke floated quietly above the tables. There was a noise of glasses and spoons. Ramón looked for something in the pocket of his old jacket. He put his wallet on the table. Look, he said. And took out a photograph.

You could see four young men. They were wearing wide trousers, light-colored shirts with the sleeves rolled up. It

must be a German summer. Behind the men it wasn't difficult to make out the shadow of some barracks. He said the
one on the right, the tallest, was Adam Mestres. Ramón's
arm was around his shoulder. He said they were all smiling
then because then wasn't yet Mathausen.

The pain the photograph spat out left the café to invade
the entrance to the church, the bakery, the tobacconist's, the
benches in the plaza. The mourning was there and nobody
even knew the name of this dead man. The grime on the
walls showed in black streaks and grayish drops.

Ramón said: Before being sent to Mathausen we four
were part of the same company. The thirty-two second, he
said. All dead, he said. We got there on April 7 in '41. They
killed Adam the following year.

He said there were times we all wanted to die because
we were already half-dead. They described Adam's death as
suicide by electrocution.

Suicide by what? Baltus asked.

Ramón said: Of course, that was the version put out by
those German animals who always confused suicide and
murder. When the SS pushed you against high-tension
wire they called it suicide. They killed Adam in front of his
father. Left him hanging on the wire like a scarecrow.

The smoke from his cigarette kept Baltus silent, his soul
watchful. He was never in a hurry. They say Baltus could
listen to people for eternity.

Ramón said when you slept on the ground there were
times when companions in the barracks died next to you,
then the dead themselves became your pillows.

He said you could die in different ways. Die in the lorry
when they transported you from one place to another. Die

in the train. Die laboring. Die in the quarry. Die thrown against the electric fences. Die executed. Die by hanging. Die drowning.

He said you could also let yourself die. He said you could also commit suicide, but when you were already worse than dead, taking your life was as difficult as trying to be blissful and starving.

He said there was a *kapo* they called Dora's Tiger.

He said that once Dora's Tiger beat a young kid so hard he killed him in front of his own father.

He said that after killing, the *kapo* went to the house and played his violin. The violin, thought Baltus. This *kapo* brought shame upon music.

In the street, Baltus stopped a tram. It took him toward the cloud over Almadora. When he got off the tram onto the lengthy pavement a dog followed him. He rang the bell to the house of roses. Nena herself opened the door.

You look miserable, she said. It gave me a fright to look at you.

When I left home this morning I didn't know what to expect. I went into the café on the plaza and met up with an old friend from La Nava. We talked and drank for hours. Then Baltus couldn't go on. He just said: Adam's dead.

The Folch ladies looked out of the front door. They were cold and hesitant about going out or not onto the marble steps. They tried to circle round Baltus. They were excited by the wedding and the continuous flow of presents to the house. We don't know where to put them all, they said.

Let's go, she said. And took the sad man off to the tool-shed.

In the toolshed, Nena held Baltus's face tight with her writer's hands. You've got to bite death hard so it can't do so much harm, she said.

Look at the rain. Look at the sky, said Nena. One had to believe the omens. The sky was a sign from Adam. If it rains, said Nena, it's good luck for the wedding. Baltus's tears tasted sweet as water. Nena drank from his face. Rain was life's unhappiness. That's why it was so necessary.

This wedding was too quick and rainy.

It was eleven A.M. when a black, high-roofed, square-shaped Ford stopped in front of the church. First the bride-groom in top hat and tails got out of the car followed by the matron of honor in mink stole and light feather hat.

A porter dressed in livery held open the doors of the cars driving up for the ceremony. He was busy welcoming guests, shielding them from the rain with an umbrella and accompanying them to the entrance to the church of the patron of the city. A crowd of bystanders had gathered with umbrellas and mackintoshes in the street of the Virgin of Mercy. When the bride arrived fifteen minutes later, the water was still pouring down but the onlookers remained impassive under the rain. First they looked at the man driving the bride's car. Then they looked at the white flurry of the bride getting out of the black car. Those with no umbrellas stuck their heads out of the doorways onto the street. They wanted a close-up of the bride's white dress, to lose their eyes in the long train of the tulle dress. She looks like a real princess, they said. The bystanders waited in the street during the whole ceremony. They were waiting for the couple to appear. A wedding like this was reason enough for a street party. Let's see the couple, they said.

As it was a cold morning and wouldn't stop raining, the guests showed off in their flashy furs and elegant hats. The wedding photographer said he'd taken a lot of photos inside the church because out here the downpour made it impossible. No guest would pose for a second in front of the camera. It's a pity, he said. When the wedding banquet began, my father came up behind me and said a cablegram had just arrived from the Vatican.

Baltus read out the telegram during the meal: His Holiness. Wishes heartfelt happiness on the newly betrothed. Baltasar Arnau and Nena Rocamora. Praying for apostolic blessing. Wishing them Christian happiness.

Nena read the lunch menu which was also, she said, in telegram style: Consommé of fowl. Eggs in mayonnaise. Lobster Cardinali. Prat chicken à la Cocotte. Viennese ice cream supreme. Wedding cake. Coffee and liqueurs. All that according to the menu.

As the couple were in mourning over Mrs. Arnau's recent death there was no dance after lunch. The banquet finished late. As it was the middle of winter, by five P.M. the sky was already dark. What's more, said Baltus, we must set out early tomorrow.

As they didn't want the train journey to Madrid to last too long, the newlyweds spoke in long sentences and words cut in half by interruptions from the steam engine. They tried to prevent the silence prolonging the minutes on the track. They ensured the silence didn't anticipate fatigue that might fall prey to boredom. In the end, Nena fell asleep with her head on Baltus's shoulder.

We sat in the first carriage. There were three people in our compartment. Two of them were from Albacete but got off in Saragossa. We watched the trees pass by like frightened green birds. The train stopped in every station imaginable, said Nena.

In Madrid they stayed in a hotel close to the Prado Museum. They spent the first day going from the Prado Museum to the hotel and from the hotel to the Prado Museum. They liked eating in a restaurant on the Gran Vía where they ordered a typical Madrid stew. They went to Chicote's. They went to the Jockey Club. They went to the Retiro. They went to Toledo. They went to the theater, they said. But didn't say they spent most of the time discovering each other. In bed.

Translated by Peter Bush

Gang Warfare

Juan Marsé

IT ALL BEGAN ONE AFTERNOON when Itchy was
setting up his used comic book stand in the Plaza del
Norte, on the sidewalk outside of Los Luises where a
blind man, sitting on a folding stool, sold lottery tickets.
The kids from Los Luises were going at a rag ball and
raising a lot of dust. It was a windy day and he looked
around for stones to hold the comic books down.
Shortly thereafter Luis arrived with his lunch under his
arm and a packet of *Merlins* and *Jorge and Fernandos:*
"Java's got another pile of *Tarzans,*" he said. "He's just
gotten them for only the price of the weight of the

JUAN MARSÉ *(Tarragona, 1933–) worked as an unskilled
worker in a jeweler's shop from 1946 to 1960. Describing himself as a
"worker-writer," he won the Planeta Prize in 1978 and the European
Literature Prize in 1994. He has created a fictional world from the
communities of migrants of the poor rural south who lived in the
industrial belt around Barcelona. This extract from his masterpiece,*
The Fallen *(1973), displays a bleak brutality that gives a twist to the
triumphalist line of Franco's Tourist Ministry's propaganda—"Spain
is different." The book wasn't published in Spain until after Franco's
death.*

paper; go right now and get them, I couldn't bring all of them." He seemed very tired and was having trouble breathing. Itchy lent him his coughdrops, and then went off to Java's and Luis stayed to watch the comic book stand, sitting with his back against the wall. He began to cough, opened the little box of coughdrops and tossed four of them into his mouth. He sold a *Mutt and Jeff* calendar for a *real* and exchanged an old *Flash Gordon* for two *Shadow* albums without covers. Itchy likes *The Shadow*, he thought to himself, he'll be happy. Only a few youngsters came over to the stand to have a look—school kids from Los Hermanos and the Divino Maestro. Some men in berets were sitting on a stone bench in the square, talking together and staring at their feet; seen from the back they seemed not to have heads. Clutching his belly as if he'd been hit by a stray bullet, one of them suddenly doubled over and fell face down in the dust. Two teaching monks from Los Hermanos who were playing soccer with their cassocks tucked up took him away to get medical treatment. "Twenty numbers being drawn today," the blind man chanted. A woman in a turban and dark glasses crossed the center of the square, waggling her hips. The wind whistled among the ruins of the dye factory on the Calle Martí and whipped the laurel peeking over the wall of the Salesians. Whirling in the dust, the blue cover of *Signal*, showing Messerschmitts diving, coiled about Luis's feet, who stood there coughing with his lunch in his hand, without having yet bitten into it: half a loaf of bread split in two with a slice of quince, hard and black as a dried fish. As he was getting ready to sink his teeth into it, with a sigh, he saw three guys with the look of bullies coming toward him. They came up to him and began pawing through the comic books but didn't buy a single one. Two more from Los Luises joined them, waving Ping-Pong paddles, and then another one he recognized: he was from the Palacio de la Cultura and had a shoebox with silkworms and mulberry leaves in his hand. They destroyed the comic book stand and tore a cover. Luis put his lunch to one side. The one with the silkworms, standing there with his legs apart, challenged him: "Who broke his arm? Which of you beat him up, you shitty slum kid?"

"What are you talking about, baby-face?"

"You know very well, you turd."

"You're the shits."

Sitting on his heels, swaying back and forth, Luis pushed the closest one and tore the comic book from his hands: "kid," he said, "they're raffling off a beating, and you've got all the winning tickets."

"Is that so? Your mother's just gone by on her way to the Bosque movie theater," the other kid said with a nasty smile. "Did you know she works the last row of the peanut gallery?"

"That whore isn't my mother."

"Yes she is, and she does jerk-off jobs, and she's got a scar on her tit."

Luis blinked in surprise, momentarily forgetting how much he'd like to blast his enemy. "A scar?" he said. "Are you sure? The woman who just went by has a scar on her breast?"

They didn't listen to him. They trampled on the stand. With one swipe of his hand Luis knocked the box with the worms to the ground. "Get that filthy thing out of here, you fairy," he said, "beat it or I'll clobber you." The other boy came a few steps closer, followed by his cohorts.

"You've got no right to talk, you lousy consumptive. And your father's in jail."

A springtime smile flowered on Luis's pale mouth, and his chest swelled.

"Because he does whatever he likes."

"Because he's a Red. That's why. And your mother does jerk-off jobs in the cinema for a peseta, and everybody knows it."

Luis stood up, his fist clenched. A painful grimace took the place of the smile.

"Say that again."

"Your mother's a jerk-off whore."

"So's yours, you son of a bitch."

Luis butted him in the balls with his head, and the other boy screamed to high heaven. They rolled on the ground together. The others leaped on top of him and made him let go of his prey, of the flesh that he was already sinking his nails and his teeth into, and they kicked him in the ribs, forced him to the ground, and twisted his arm behind his back. They hit him in the nape of the neck and his sides with the handles of the Ping-Pong paddles. The blind man turned his wooden face in the direction of the blows, his profile rigid, obstinate: "Drawing today," he chanted. The row went on without a let-up in the middle of the square. The men sitting on the bench watched the fight with teary eyes full of dust, and no one moved, none of them came over to separate them.

"This is for what you did to Miguel," the one with the melodious voice said to him, kicking him. "And this, and this."

When they let go of him he lay there on all fours, suck-ing his split lip with his tongue, coughing. He picked up the comic books torn to shreds and the remainder of his lunch. He felt he was about to vomit and covered his mouth with his hand, as the warm blood came trickling through his fingers.

He went running to the junk shop, wanting to tell Java: they've seen her in the Bosque, they've touched her scar. Before he got there, at the public tap in the Calle Camelias, on the corner of Escorial, he stuck his head under the flow-ing water. He began coughing again then, and his chest hurt so much he had to lean his back against the wall. He was breathing like a bellows, his face was deathly pale, and with his bulging eyes he could not see or answer the person who stopped to ask him, "What's the matter, son, why don't you go home?" It was an unkempt old lady in men's shoes. A flower of blood left smudges on Luis's lips. With his eyes closed he let those anonymous hands stroke his head, he let himself be scolded gently. "They've insulted my mother," he said until the old lady left him and went on her way, mut-tering hoarse recriminations. Luis finally made it to the junk shop and told Java and Itchy what had happened in the Plaza del Norte. Amén was also there, and Java sent him running in search of the rest: first we'll settle accounts with those damned pansies and then we'll see if it's true that it was really her. Half an hour later they were all in the Plaza del Norte with their mufflers crossed over their chests like two cartridge belts and their pockets full of stones, but the enemy had gone to the Can Compte vacant lot in search of ammunition. They caught up with their adversaries there. They attacked them with a rain of stones and saw them take to their heels but they weren't able to catch a single one of them; they reappeared later with reinforcements from Los Luises and the battle lasted till nightfall along Alegre de Dalt, Balcells, and Martí, outside the Remedio Clinic, whose high walls bristled with glass shards and sharpened bits of bottles. The neighbors closed their windows and balconies; it was one of the bloodiest stone fights in memory. Itchy got hit on the forehead with a stone and went around with a bandage around his head for a month. Amén skinned a knee and Martín twisted an ankle. The one who came off worst of all was Mingo: as he was leaping over the wall of the clinic he slipped, catching his pants on the shards of glass, and remaining hung up there for a moment, finding a handhold wherever he could. He kicked and tried to jerk himself free, and they saw him hanging there with his wrist caught on a piece of glass as sharp as a stiletto, which finally broke. So much blood spurted out that they thought he'd cut his veins. They took him to a dispensary, and at the jewelery shop where he worked they had to fire him, and he was going about now with his arm in a sling and a bandage over his forehead, looking like a young lead in a movie, a wounded Prisoner of Zenda.

Translated by Helen Lane

Is Angela There?

Carme Riera

HANDS FOLDED, the stocking on the table cast aside
for now—on account of the third commandment—she
peered through the window's polyester curtains, dusty and
dirtied by grubby fingers. There was hardly anyone out on
the street. She could hear the cars and buses on the road,
though, the rumble of the Ramblas, right there by her
house. Shame that tall, ugly building blocked her view of
the passersby: young girls, old women leaving mass, people lining up outside the movie theater box office, lovers,
children. . . . Some Sundays she felt an almost irresistible
urge just to go and sit on a bench and while away the

CARME RIERA *(Palma de Mallorca, 1948–) is one of
Catalunya's best-known women writers. A professor at the Universi-
tat Autònoma de Barcelona, she has published numerous novels as well
as short stories and scholarly works. She has won many literary prizes
for her novels* Una primavera per a Domenico Guarini, Joc de
miralls, *and* Dins el darrer blau, *a historical novel about the
Inquisition in Mallorca. Riera is known for using dialect and popular
speech without condescension. "Is Angela There?," from her 1975 book of
short stories,* Te deix, amor, la mar com a penyora, *is written in the
Mallorcan dialect of Catalan.*

evening, watching folks walk by. But the possible shame of being caught by an acquaintance, sitting there all alone, surveying the scene, held her back. So she resigned herself to peering through the window. She stared up the street, trying to make out the gender of a sprawled figure, the color and shape of its clothes. This undertaking kept her faintly amused. When no one was walking by, she inspected the facades of the buildings, giving them a good once-over. She knew all the cracks in the walls by heart, the colors of everyone's shutters ("Tomeu the stonemason painted his but two weeks ago and they're fading already"), the dark oil spots on the asphalt. . . .

Staring down at the lonely street—thirty meters long, four meters wide, litter strewn on the ground, old apartment buildings—she decided, every Sunday afternoon, that she didn't like Sundays. The maid left early, right after lunch, and didn't come back until nightfall. The neighbors left, too, and the three-story building felt abandoned. Any old thief who'd been keeping watch on the place, hiding in a doorway, could have snuck in when the coast was clear and made off with whatever he liked, easy as you please, without raising the slightest suspicion. She was scared and never felt safe, despite the many chains, bolts, and locks on her apartment door. Creaking furniture and dripping water (the laundry-room faucet leaked) startled her immeasurably. Weekdays were much more pleasant: she'd grumble along with the maid, listen to the kids upstairs fighting, to the voice of the neighbor across the landing, who often sang:

> *Yo que siempre de los hombres me burlé,*
> *Yo que siempre de los hombres me reí,*

Yo que nunca sus palabras escuché,
Hoy en busca de un amante vengo aquí.
¡Ay de mí! ¡Ay de mí! . . .

When she peered through the window—the needles between her fingers bobbing up and down as she knit a pink shawl—she did it secure in the knowledge that she would see the same people at the same times: office workers, youngsters on their way to and from school—she had a soft spot for the Rovira twins—apprentices from the dressmaker's shop two streets up, and even a couple of civil guards, *ses senyores civiles*, who by and large spent the afternoons out on patrol. This routine gave her a sense of security. She knew the faces and clothes of all those folks. She could, with almost no effort, guess where they were off to or where they were coming from, what they were doing, what kind of moods they were in. She would have liked to invite them up for a spell, for coffee and Mallorcan pastries, just to see if they had the voices she imagined. After mulling it over for a good long time, one day she decided to try her luck. She summoned up enough courage to wave at a young girl who for some time now had been passing by twice—at four and seven—every afternoon. What harm could there be, after all? So with a kindly expression, she smiled down at the youngster to let her know she was beckoning her. But things didn't turn out according to plan, and she was in for a dreadful shock: the wicked child was a sassy little thing and just stuck out her tongue before flouncing off, cool as you please.

This incident made her lose the faith she had been building—for no real reason—in the inherent good nature of her clockwork friends, and it played a big part in her decision to change the way she lived her life.

Although she still enjoyed peering through the window, she began to look on her pastime as dangerous. She was afraid that folks who until then had passed by almost unaware of her presence would realize she was spying on them—though she had no evil intentions, of course. The idea of bumping into Little Miss Sassy upset her awfully, too, and she was afraid that the other children, the civil guards, and the office workers would all start to gibe and point when she least expected it.

Her only choice was to come up with another pursuit, one that would distance her from folks yet still keep her in touch with them. That was when, hopeful of finding a solution, she decided to buy herself a telephone. It fit all her specifications: she could dial a number—any one of thousands, in fact—and be put into contact with others, but remain anonymous and even invisible.

She commenced. Her wrinkled fingers traced little circles on the dial; then came an intermittent ringing. After a while, seconds, minutes, someone answered at the other end of the line.

—Hello? Hello? Yes? Hello? . . .

She listened to all the voices carefully. She'd guess their moods by the tone, picking up on almost imperceptible subtleties.

—Hello? (Businessman, probably about forty, married, children . . .)

—Hello, is Angela there?

—You have the wrong number, ma'am.

—Oh, I'm sorry. I must have misdialed. . . .

And she'd hang up. And call someone else: six numbers dialed at random but filling a need. A few seconds and then the unfamiliar voice:

—Hello?

—Hello, is Angela there, by chance?

—Who?

—Angela. May I speak to her?

—You have the wrong number, ma'am. There's no Angela here.

—But this is the number she gave me!

—All the same, I can assure you she doesn't live here. . . .

Sometimes she'd ring the same number two or three times, driving to distraction the person who answered. And that's how she spent most afternoons, especially Sunday afternoons: sitting by the phone, lifting the receiver over and over again. She knew before dialing what part of the city the house would be in, since she consulted the phone book now and again for that sort of information. And when she tired of inventing arithmetic sequences, she'd run her index finger up and down a page with her eyes closed, not opening them until it came to rest; wherever her finger was pointing, that was the lucky number.

She always asked for the same person: Angela, Doña Angela, or Miss Angela, depending on the degree of kinship or affinity she thought might exist between her imagined friend and the person who answered the phone. Because, of course, Angela had grown into a friend she desperately wanted to talk to—getting on in years, dark eyes, a spinster or maybe a widow, an old hand at crochet—and one day it happened.

—Hello?

—Is Angela home, by chance?

—Well, I believe she's just getting ready to go out. Just a second, I'll go and see. . . . She's coming.

And then:

—Hello?

—Angela?

—Is that you, Maria?

—Yes.

—Oh, I'm sorry, dear; I didn't recognize your voice.

—I know, I'm a little stuffed up.

—I can tell. You sound funny.

—I think I'm coming down with the flu. I'm sorry to bother you; I know you were just getting ready to go out. . . .

—Well, I should hope you know. We're meeting at six and it's a quarter to now. Are you ready?

—Well, you see, I don't think it's a good idea for me to go out. . . .

—But why didn't you call me earlier? Now what am I going to do with the tickets?

It was getting tricky but—with great care and a surprising degree of composure—she tried to follow Angela's lead, prepared to pick up on any idea she could.

—It's probably too late to return them. What time did you say it was?

—Quarter to six.

—Oh. Well, don't worry; I'll pay you for them.

—That's not what I meant. I just hate to see them go to waste. You can understand me not wanting to go on my own. And now it's too late to give them to anyone else. Pity you didn't let me know earlier.

—I'm sorry, but I thought that a couple of aspirins would get rid of my headache, so I put it off till the last minute.

—Well, you ought to get off the phone. I'll come by and see you in an hour. Do you need anything?

—No, I'm fine. But thank you for coming. I really appreciate it.

—Don't be silly, dear! What else would I do?

—Okay, well, see you in a little while, then.

—Bye.

—Bye now.

And she hung up. Angela! She had found Angela, and Angela was coming to see her. She would straighten up the living room a bit. No, the living room didn't need it, the bedroom. She'd put on a fresh bedspread, but first she'd iron it a little; it was all wrinkled up after being in the cupboard for so long. Shame not to have finished that pink shawl—now that she didn't peer out the window anymore, she hardly knitted at all. She would brush out her curls since she didn't have time to wash her hair. She'd pick out a nightgown and get into bed, with her robe at her feet so she could throw it on quickly, the moment she heard the doorbell.

An hour sped by. She tidied up her room: all the clothes draped over chairs, the sheets behind the bed disappeared, hung up in the armoire and carefully placed in boxes. She put on the fresh bedspread; it looked lovely. It was a little uneven on one side, but if you weren't looking for it, you'd never know. She fixed up her hair a bit: there was no doubt that a bun favored her more than any other style, and besides it hid all the tangles. She chose a nightgown—it had been her mother's but she never wore it—it was linen, very fine linen. She climbed into bed. It was almost seven. Angela would be there any minute.

She looked around the room. Would Angela like it? She got up; with all the rushing, she had forgotten to take the aspirin for her headache. She went into the kitchen for a glass of water—she'd get it straight from the tap; the water in the fridge was too cold and would be no good for the flu—and swallowed both pills down in one gulp. She went back to the bedroom with the jar and the glass; she left them on the nightstand and climbed back into bed.

Half past seven. What a slowpoke, that Angela! Could something have happened to her? The minutes dragged by. Should I count sheep? No, I'm not trying to fall asleep. She got up again. I'll unlock the door: it wouldn't be right to make Angela wait. Besides, what would she say if she heard all that noise behind the door? The burglar won't come today, and anyhow, with Angela here I won't be all alone. There will be two of us, and even if we can't defend ourselves, we can at least scream. . . .

Eight o'clock. Half past. No sign of Angela. She began to get angry. She probably wouldn't even come at this rate. Why, Angela had tricked her! But no, of course, it was her own fault. How could Angela come if she didn't even have her address? She ran to the phone; maybe it wasn't too late. She dialed a number; she waited. Finally, a voice:

—Hello?

—Angela?

—You have the wrong number, ma'am, there's no Angela here.

—But I phoned just a little while ago and spoke to her.

—That must have been another number.

She insisted.

—Would you please tell Angela she has a telephone call?

—I already told you, you have the wrong number.

And again.

—Listen, please could you just do me this favor and go and tell doña Angela . . . ?

Her voice trembled.

—I repeat, madam, wrong number.

—It is not the wrong number. I don't know why you don't just go and tell her. It's urgent!

—Lady, go to hell! And don't bother me again.

Desperate, she phoned another number: a horrible, intermittent busy signal assaulted her ears. There was nothing she could do about it.

Days passed. She carried on with stubborn determination and always got the same result: wrong number. In the end she realized that, plainly, she had forgotten Angela's number after that Sunday-afternoon conversation. But she resolved to keep trying her luck and spent her days and part of her nights on the phone, inquiring relentlessly:

—Is Angela there, by chance?

Translated from the Catalan by Lisa Dillman

The Five Doorstops

Quim Monzó

AS SUMMER WAS IN THE AIR, so were the summer holidays, and Berta decided to buy five doorstops for the five inside doors in the house she and her husband owned by the beach. It was no spur-of-the-moment decision. Every summer, when she opened the doors to let in some fresh air, and there was a strong draft, the doors banged, the glass panes clattered, and some shattered. Every year, after the first bangs, to avoid any repeat, she'd wedge flowerpots or chairs against the doors, but it was evident that, albeit a temporary fix, the pots and chairs provided no definitive solution. Consequently every August she decided that as soon as she was back in Barcelona she'd buy five stops to avoid a repeat performance the following year. In mid-August the need seemed so urgent she even contemplated going to Barcelona for a day to buy the

QUIM MONZÓ *(Barcelona, 1952–) is a leading Catalan writer of his generation and has won the National Prize for Catalan Literature and numerous other literary awards. This story is from his most recent collection,* El millor dels mons. *Novelist Robert Coover has described him as "the most amusing Catalan writer I've read."*

stops and come back straightaway. If she never did, it was because the shops she knew were shut, and it would have been a real odyssey to find five stops elsewhere. But back in Barcelona in September, the sense of urgency waned and she postponed her purchases; so on her return the following summer, no sooner had she entered their beach house, than she remembered she hadn't bought the doorstops the previous September, or in any subsequent month. That oscillation between urgent necessity and oblivion was helped by the fact that in winter—from November and particularly around Christmas—when they went to the house, the cold meant the doors were always closed and there was no need for any stops.

But this year she decided that this August she didn't want to arrive and lament yet again their lack of wedges. So on a mid-morning in June she went out intent on making a purchase. In the first home decoration shop where she stopped—a fussy little shop, with windows polished with emory paper and varnished wooden walls—the owner announced, in a tone of voice Berta judged to be slightly haughty, that she no longer had any. They'd had some years ago, the woman continued, but not any more. Berta had been in this shop, as an adolescent, one afternoon when her mother had fetched her from school.

"Will you be getting more in?"

The woman clicked her tongue, as if Berta had asked something beyond the pale.

"Nobody uses them nowadays."

The second shop, only recently opened, told her they'd never stocked any such thing. In the third, the shopkeeper curled her lip and looked bewildered.

"Some what?"

"Some doorstops. You know what I mean? They're wedges, stops, you put them under doors to stop them from moving when they're open, to stop them from banging when there's a draft."

"Oh!" replied the shopkeeper. She led her to a shelf and pointed to some round rubber stops.

The fourth shop did have some. They were a dark, shiny wood, animated by a lurid, elaborate snail design. She could never buy them. She had better luck in the fifth shop, which sold two makes: one set was wrought iron and adorned with a mouse; the other, made of plastic, was simple, broad, and gently inclined for easy insertion, whatever size the gap between door and floor. They were signed: *Design: Berto Pandolfo*.

Back home she tried one out. Slotted it under a door and tried to open it. No way. She only had to put them in place, not even squeeze them underneath and the doors were immobilized: though made of a light plastic material, their ample length and width prevented any movement, however strong the draft. On the other hand, you could easily extract them. Delighted, she returned them to their packet.

After dinner when it was dark, she decided to show them to Victor. Victor grabbed one, looking really astonished, scrutinized it closely, and immediately got up to test it out on the nearest door. Berta tried to stop him—"Wait a minute!" but too late: despite her plea, Victor was already forcing it in, using all the strength of the arms of an ex-champion gymnast, with silver and gold medals on the parallel bars from two Olympic Games. To round the job off, he kicked it a couple of times. Berta was in the middle of the dining room, her eyes bulging, one hand clasped over her mouth to prevent herself from screaming.

"Not like that!"

"Yes," he replied. "Just like that. Otherwise, the draft will dislodge them. They're only plastic."

Berta ran toward the stop. When she finally extricated it—because he'd jammed it tight—she contemplated the result. Because he'd placed it on the slant and kicked it a couple of times, the edge of the door had scraped the top of the stop, which was designed to be inserted straight, not on the slant. It now displayed a deep incision that was both lamentable and unnecessary. Berta couldn't shake off her state of shock.

"There was no need to kick it! You just place them gently under the door, and they stay put."

Berta couldn't keep her eyes off the incision; couldn't understand why. She was in a rage. Tears welled up and she fought them off so she didn't seem so hurt, so Victor couldn't derive pleasure from her discomfort. How could he be so careless, so unintelligent as not to see the perfectly conceived shape of a stop that required no force at all? That was its beauty. Besides, why had he forced it in on the *slant?* Whatever might he'd applied, if he'd inserted it at right angles to the door, its generous width would have let it withstand any onslaught, and it wouldn't have been damaged. She took a deep breath because she felt her heart beat too rapidly. Her rage wasn't disproportionate. It was no trivial act, Berta realized, Berta who was still in the passageway by the door, ensuring Victor didn't see her bloodshot eyes. It was no trivial act, she noted again. It wasn't the first time; something similar had happened only two months ago. She'd brought a bouquet of dried flowers home, red roses with the most delicate, brittle petals and leaves. She'd taken a taxi so they didn't get knocked in the bus and, once home, she'd carefully arranged them in a vase. On a low table, in the lounge. What did Victor do? When he came in he hadn't even notice them. But when she asked him if he liked the flowers she'd brought, he looked at them for the first time, wiped away an insipid smile, pounced on the vase and rearranged the stems—as if they didn't look perfect!—and so roughly that petals and leaves fell off; when he'd finished, the whole table was covered. Berta held back her tears on that occasion too.

Victor had been seated at the table for some time. He turned up the volume on the television with the remote control and recalled that morning at the beach house last summer, when the sun beat down on the console wall and, in the distance, over the noise of the waves, floated the laughter of children who'd just got their fringes wet. The more they tried to have a child, the more time they devoted to the task, the more children he thought he saw in the street, on balconies, crying in neighboring apartments. That day he'd contemplated how the terrace roofs fanned out under the bluest of skies. At the very moment he'd turned to come inside, Victor had noticed the cord to the blind. It was one of those imitation wood blinds, which are usually kept up by tying the cord to a hook in the window frame. Victor stared: the cord was tied to the hook not with a neat bow but a knot: a big, ugly knot that had been tied time and again.

It wasn't easy. His nails weren't long enough and Berta

had pulled it so tight it took him a while to undo the first knot. Then the second and the third. There was even a fourth. When he finally undid the last one, the cord, which was also plastic, looked like a crumpled streamer. It had looked like that for some time. How often had he told her that, to keep the blind up, there was no need to knot the cord, a simple bow would suffice? A bow would keep the blind in place, and the cord wouldn't crumple. On the contrary, a gentle tug on the cord undid the bow. Knots spoiled the cord and hitched it on the hook. Besides, why *four* big knots?

That night, when Berta noticed Victor pretending to come inside her—and immediately withdrawing and spilling his seed on the sly over the sheet—she realized it was his response to a slight he'd suffered at her hands that day, but she never thought for one moment it had to do with the knot on the blind cord. She often wondered: why did he sometimes punish her by pretending to moan when he was inside her and when he only ejaculated afterward once he'd come out? Hadn't they decided they wanted a child? He did it more and more; to deprive him of the pleasure of seeing her annoyance, she pretended not to notice and said: "I can feel your hot milk. What shall we call him?"

"If it's a boy, Marc; if it's a girl, Silvia," he'd reply.

"No," insisted Berta. "If it's a boy, Victor, like you . . ."

Victor didn't like his name one bit: perhaps that's why she'd said that. He liked it as little as she liked his habit of immediately lighting a cigarette—the whole ritual, flourish of hands, lighter, first drag, and puff of smoke—only to abandon it in the ashtray. He was always doing that, and not just in bed. Gradually, the cigarette burned and by the time he'd remembered, it was a coil of ash. He'd look rather upset, as if surprised it had disappeared so quickly. As there wasn't one drag left, he'd flatten it with a grimace and repeat the exact same ritual with another cigarette: lighting up with all the effects and then abandoning it in the ashtray. You didn't have to be a genius to conclude that Victor liked to light up, not to smoke. This custom irritated Berta even more when the cigarette lay in the groove of the ashtray, precariously balanced so that, as the half inside the ashtray turned to ash, the weight of the unburnt cigarette tipped it out, till finally it fell on the table or tablecloth, burning the table or the material, or both.

Victor didn't like to smoke and wouldn't have lit up and let the cigarettes burn so assiduously if it hadn't annoyed Berta. He'd noticed it straightaway, the first night they'd gone out, many summers ago. They'd dined and after dessert, Victor caught Berta looking irritated at the cigarette he'd abandoned in the ashtray. He lit up because he was nervous, because dining with her made him happy, yet at the same time he was afraid there wouldn't be a second time. He was in love and wanted to tell her and didn't know if he should or not and, should he decide to, in what way, with which words, and when exactly. And, as he never smoked, he'd lit the cigarette and, not knowing what to do after the second puff, he'd left it in the ashtray. Till it burned away. Afterward he'd extinguished it and lit up another. By the time their coffee came, a fourth cigarette was smoking away. Victor also stared and saw how absurdly it disappeared without even a puff from him. Until that fourth cigarette he'd not realized how much it riled Berta, but he was really pleased it was so because it riled him that during the whole meal Berta methodically ate only half of each course. She lifted her fork once or twice to her mouth, three or four times at most, and then put knife and fork across a half-full plate. She followed suit with first and second courses and dessert. Victor thought hers a disdainful, snobbish attitude. Victor never discovered that Berta also did it because she was nervous, that nerves had taken her appetite away and that, if she hadn't forced herself, she wouldn't even have eaten half of each course. Wouldn't have downed a mouthful. Till she'd crossed knife and fork on the second plate, she'd not noticed Victor's irritation, and then she decided to make a routine of it. Neither did Victor ever discover that the decisive factor determining their second date was the fact that later on, as they were saying good-bye in the porch to her house, to get a better kiss Victor had placed an open hand on the white wall—an open hand on a white wall!— and when he removed it, he left five finger marks. The marks were so slight no one would have noticed them if they'd not been pointed out and one had the time and determination to take a closer look. But Berta could see the sweat marks of someone so unthoughtful as to put an open hand on a white wall. From such a perspective Berta could hardly not agree, if rather anxiously, when Victor suggested they met a second time.

Translated from the Catalan by Peter Bush

School Memory

Bernardo Atxaga

WE LOOKED PERFECTLY ANGELIC in our end-of-term photographs, but Teacher, who was born in a land far away from the Basque Country and dreamed of entering the military profession, knew full well that the opposite was true. We kids, by order of our elder brothers, refused to salute the Spanish flag that waved, red and gold, over the schoolhouse; we purposely garbled the words of the fascist hymn "Cara al sol"; and we spent our morning classes planning the boxing matches that, in the spirit of the Cassius Clay–Sonny Liston fight of that year, 1964, would take place during recess.

BERNARDO ATXAGA *(Asteasu, 1951–) is the pseudonym of José Irazu Garmendia. In his early professional life he was an economist, teacher of Basque (Euskera), bookseller, printer, radio scriptwriter, and more. From the early 1980s he decided to concentrate on his writing and won national and international recognition with the publication of the novel* Obabakoak, *which won the National Literature Prize in 1989 and has been translated into more than twenty languages. He writes in Euskera and usually translates his own work into Spanish. He has recently been Visiting Professor at Harvard University. This story was published in the newspaper,* El Heraldo de Aragón.

"They're a bunch of little savages," Teacher reported to the school inspector who had come to impose order. "If I don't intervene, they'll end up killing each other."

"What are they up to, then?" asked the inspector scanning the dozen or so rows of school desks, seated at which, among others, were the fierce Areta, Opin the gruff, and above all, the indomitable Andrés, better known as Chessman.

"These children hate each other," declared Teacher. "The minute they go out for recess they start fighting like wild animals. It's frightening. I've never seen anything like it before."

Teacher, I realize now, must have been a weak and inexperienced young man, hardly the Soldado Español he claimed to be whenever anyone enquired about his high leather boots and his thick buckled belt. Otherwise he would never have kept silent about our graver sin—patriotic indifference.

"Which one of them is the ringleader?" asked the inspector, nervously pacing around the teacher's platform. We noticed that he took off his wedding ring and left it on the desk.

We were all certain that Teacher would name either the fierce Areta, Opin the gruff, or the indomitable Andrés, better known as Chessman.

"The dark one sitting by the window," said our teacher, pointing in the direction of Azpetitxe.

"Come here you little wretch!" screamed the inspector in a more strident tone that scared me, sitting in the front row with the smaller kids.

"Do you know why I've taken my ring off?" he asked us

then. "So that my blows won't leave marks on the face of this rebel."

No sooner were the words out of his mouth than the first whack, a startling backhand, reverberated against Azpetitxe's cheek.

The exemplary punishment had begun.

Azpetitxe was one of those isolated students, a lonely child. He wasn't from Obaba, but from the neighboring town of Azpeitia. Hence his nickname, Azpetitxe. He had arrived at our school months after the term began, and by then it was too late to make new friends or join one of the village gangs. Then too, he was a little strange, and what we found most troubling about him, what pained us the most, was his stubbornness in a fight, his total unwillingness to cry. During the boxing matches at recess—which were conducted on a first-tears basis, ending when one of the contenders admitted defeat and started to cry—everyone avoided him, except, of course, the indomitable Chessman. It was widely understood that Azpetitxe only understood voids or victories.

Nor was he to be defeated that day. The inspector wore himself out with blow after blow, until his morals and his Catholic principles were stretched to the limit, and still he didn't get the better of Azpetitxe's will. The boy's nose was bleeding, but there was no trace of tears on his face. Only a smirk, the shadow of a smile.

"I think that will suffice, Señor Inspector," said Teacher. He had turned very pale. There was absolute silence in the classroom now, and all eyes were upon Azpetitxe. He was good, he was even better than the indomitable Chessman.

"Sit down!" screamed the inspector. But again, it was a

different voice. He had been defeated. He put his ring back on his finger and hurried toward the exit, averting his eyes, like a thief. At the other end of the classroom, Azpetitxe straightened himself up, smiling widely as his deskmate slapped him admiringly on the back.

"Now you know what will happen to you if this sort of behavior continues," threatened the inspector from the doorway. "Yes, now you know," he repeated as he closed the door, mumbling to himself as though about to faint.

No one turned around. Let him go, that pig, and good riddance. As the indomitable Chessman said, in a perfectly audible whisper, "Adiós, brute."

Translated by Amaia Gabantxo

Your Gernika

Amaia Gabantxo

SHE SCRUBBED THE WOODEN TABLES with a hard, wiry brush, her hands reddened raw from the bleach. She scrubbed and the tables danced irritatingly on the uneven floor. She was angry. She scrubbed faster and faster.

She walked out from the smell of bleach and the bottles of beer and wine and the loaves of bread behind the bright blue counter. She dried her hands on her apron, tucking her hair back under her headscarf. It was a beautiful morning, late April, and the sky was blue. The light flooded the bay. The primary colors of the few boats anchored in the port demanded to be looked at. The greens greened, the reds reddened.

The stone bench where she sat and cried that day is still here. I've sat on it often, as a child, as a teenager, before I ever knew how long it had been there, before I ever looked

AMAIA GABANTXO *(1973–) was born in the Basque Country, where she grew up speaking both Basque and Spanish. She moved to England at age 20, and began to write in English. She now lives in Norwich, teaching literature at the University of East Anglia and writing reviews for the* Times Literary Supplement. *She is currently working on a novel dealing with fragmentation of identity and memory.*

at it with the eyes of memory and realized ghosts sat on it. It offers a commanding view of the island and of the estuary that opens softly at its feet. The blond beach that insinuates itself in the distance, the silver rock that guards it. So that day she sat and silently cried out her impotence and her anger. She sat and wondered how long before she'd lose her job. For three months now she had managed to ward off her boss's advances; soon it would be over, one way or another.

Earlier, he had cornered and fondled her, had demanded that she undo her shirt buttons and show him her generous cleavage. Then he had laughed at her and ordered her to bring more beer bottles up from the cellar.

At first she seems just increasingly eccentric. Then someone utters the word, first in a whisper, then in trembling fear, finally in despair. Alzheimer's. Her memory disappears slowly, tiny strokes in her brain destroying neurons, blacking out spaces, sections, events, people dead and alive. In the kitchen, she sits after breakfast and demands that lunch be made ready for her husband, my grandfather, long dead. My mother distracts her with some seeds that need sorting, some knitting, some sewing or ironing. Soon even that becomes too much, and piles of ironed sheets are placed on her lap. Or she is asked to sit still minding her child, a bald-headed plastic baby.

The landlady came out and sat next to her and held her hand between hers. "Don't cry, *laztana*. He screams a lot, but that's really all there is to him. You shouldn't let him frighten you. Do you see me being frightened of him? No, you don't, and I'm his wife. I should know whether I need to be frightened of him or not, after all these years. Really, you don't need to cry. He won't do anything to you. He only screams. Let him scream! You just get on with your work. I've no complaint about you, believe me. You're a good girl and you work hard."

She knew she couldn't tell the landlady. She would certainly lose her job then. Instead, she said she was upset because she had argued with her boyfriend the night before. She knew the landlady liked to hear a bit of gossip, to feel trusted. Better to distract her from all dangerous thoughts of the tears having anything to do with her husband.

In the heat you can hear the dry bean plants cracking. The pods have to be picked. It is becoming too hot.

I love the high, tangled maze of plants, the smell of the crumbling soil, the sounds of the flies and the trickling river. I sometimes think reality gains a new dimension when we work the land, simply because that is what my ancestors did, that is how they lived, while for me this is some kind of exotic luxury.

Hands on, feeling for the dangling yellowing bean pods, happy in the shadow of the plants. Corridors of plants and wicker baskets waiting to be filled.

My grandmother is with me in the field. This is one of the things she can still do, if slowly. I work my way through the bean plants, enjoying the slight breeze that ruffles the leaves, the baskets that shine in the light for me, as I leave them behind, full. I gather the beans in my apron and then throw them into the baskets. I think of locusts as I let them fall.

I can hear my grandmother's voice. As I come closer I

can hear she is calling her dead sister's name. "Estefana, Estefana," she is calling. She sounds happy and carefree. "Come and see this, come quick." She looks up at me, smiling, and shushes me. She points at a crevice of green where it seems my aunt's cat has just delivered her litter. "We won't tell anyone," she says, and she holds a finger to her mouth.

How old is she today, I wonder. Perhaps twelve years old, summer of 1928. With her sister, she is picking bean pods on her father's farm. This hot summer's day I am Estefana. I close my eyes and join in this fantastic illusion.

"What were you telling my wife out there?"

The question rasped in her ear as her wrist numbed withpain. "Nothing. I haven't told her. I swear I haven't. Let me go."

She felt her rising anger as heat in her face and a hammering in her skull and fingertips. And like a bull, galloping in fear and anger, this anger was unstoppable. She could smell him, this beast, his sweat, his horrible breath on her neck. She could smell her own humiliation, her embarrassed silences.

"You know, girl, you work here because I want you to. And I think your mother won't be too happy if you lose your job. Your brothers and sisters need the money you earn." And the grip was tighter. And the breath was closer, so close now that she could hear his breathing whistling through the gaps between his teeth. So she relaxed. She knew she could not possibly win. Why fight?

Slowly, she took her apron off and released her hair from her headscarf. She stepped out of her espadrilles and lifted her skirt to show him the most beautiful pair of legs in the province. While he gawped, she took two steps forward and slapped him with all her strength, humiliation, tears, passion, embarrassment, anger, tiredness, fear, hatred. Because this particular war was lost, and her side was losing the other one too. Then she walked back into her espadrilles.

Frightened by what she had just done, trembling but happy somehow, knowing that it had been right, she sat on the stone bench and breathed deeply, shaking away the last few particles of anger.

She breathed in her triumph, her freedom. She looked up at the blue sky, such a beautiful limpid blue, so soothing.

First came the sound, like nothing she had heard before, filling the air, all the breathing space. Then she saw them. Planes. Ten, twenty, thirty, more. Gray, with swastikas on their wings, penetrating the estuary. The atmosphere trembled. Everything, her vision. She was crying. She knew, something within her knew already. And she screamed like a mother cradling a dead child in her arms.

I look into your green eyes. I hold your hand, freckled and veiny, warm and shaking. I am sitting here, I am waiting, I will stay and look into your eyes until I understand. Until you give me the signal. I know you will.

"Grandma," I say.

"Yes," you answer.

And there is no more. You stare at the colored wooden shapes placed in front of you for your entertainment.

I kiss your hand and place it on my cheek. They don't have to be words. It could be anything else. Look into my eyes. Say my name. Change the way I feel.

Your eyes fill with tears.

"Can you hear?" you say.

"No, Grandma, what is it?"

"Listen."

I strain to hear. I can't hear. Whatever it is that you are hearing is only in your mind. Now tears are streaming down your face, wetting your hands and mine.

"Children crying."

First the rumbling, then the smoke. It went on and on. Later, the planes left as they had come. Deafening, deathly.

The stone bench felt cold, like marble. Hard, constraining, like a coffin.

"What's happening? What is it? What is it?" The landlady approached her, trembling all over, suddenly a hundred years old. "Tell me, *laztantxu*. What are they doing?"

She held her in her arms, trying to comfort her, holding her to hold herself.

"Bombs. They're bombing. . . ."

They wailed. And everyone waited. They gathered blankets, they tore sheets, they made beds up in all the available spaces. They prepared cauldrons of soup that they salted with tears. They wailed and waited and, slowly, it started.

Slowly, as the distance shrank between her and the refugees carrying whatever little they had managed to rescue. Slowly, as the wailing mothers with their dead children approached, as the lamp-carrying orphans came closer, as the mutilated dragged themselves toward her.

In the quiet, in the growing darkness, she could see the glow of the distant town on fire. The glow crawled toward them, inch by inch torchbearers filled the air with flames, smoke, and their pain, their dead. Their lament grew louder and closer. All she could do was listen to this lament, listen to it grow and overtake every single emotion in her mind. She could not cry. She could only listen. And wait.

The night closed in but she did not sleep.

She no longer speaks. She just sits in her wheelchair, staring with immeasurable sadness out of the window. Her hand tightly grips whoever is sitting closest to her. If that person is me, I look out toward the hills with the same sadness and then whisper into her eyes, "I remember."

The Armoire

Carlos Blanco Aguinaga

THE STORY BEGINS on the day my mother came up
with the idea: maybe an armoire was just what she and my
father needed in the bedroom. We were just sitting down
to eat and, since you'd have trouble fitting a piece of furniture that size into an apartment with three bedrooms, a
kitchen, and a bathroom (the balcony was just to hang out
the wash and gaze out at the mountain and the estuary),
my grandfather looked shocked, while my father carried
on with his soup as if nothing had happened. Later, when
he was peeling an apple for dessert, grandfather asked
what for. My mother returned the question: What for,

CARLOS BLANCO AGUINAGA *(1926–) was born in Irún
and exiled to Mexico as a child after the Spanish Civil War. Since
earning his Ph.D., he has taught at Mexico's UNAM, the University
of California, and in Spain. The author of books on Unamuno, Pra-
dos, Marxist literary theory, and modernism, he has also published four
novels and a book of short stories,* Carretera de Cuernavaca
*(Alfaguara 1990), from which "The Armoire" was taken. The story
paints a portrait of a young boy's life in Irún just before the civil war
reaches the area. Since the town lies on the French border, the early Fascist victory there in 1936 isolated the Basque Country from France.*

what? The armoire, grandpa answered. Ah. And then my father explained that it was always better to store clothes in a good armoire than behind a curtain, an armoire like the one you have in your bedroom. I think we'd have enough to pay for it, he added. Then, over the course of the next several days, they worked out all the details. And it was grandfather himself who spoke to Etxepare about what kind of wood, the approximate size, the likely price—the fundamentals.

Etxepare had his workshop on the ground floor of our building and, as everyone knew, he was the best carpenter and cabinetmaker in town. In the whole province, some said. Everything he ever made—they said—was sturdy, impeccably finished, and lasted more than a lifetime. So great was Etxepare's fame, such his technique (always silent, intense, always wearing that beret), that friends and acquaintances regularly stopped to watch him work when they were passing by the workshop. If two or three people were strolling by and chatting, they'd greet him and then fall silent. They'd stare quietly for a few minutes and then, as they went on their way, before resuming their conversations, they'd say, Now that's a carpenter!

Same with us, the neighborhood kids. When we got tired of kicking a ball around, or playing ring-toss or tops, or shouting and climbing trees, we'd slowly wander over to the workshop door, sit on the floor at a discreet distance and, without opening our mouths, we'd watch, entranced by Etxepare's movements. We were especially in awe of his pauses: he would put his hand on his waist, push back his beret to scratch his head, survey or caress whatever he was making, then look over the whole workshop inch by inch, pull his beret back down, think a little more and, whistling lightly, go back to work. When we were all running to the fountain later, I would brag that Etxepare's workshop was in the same building as my house.

Even better than that was a mystery, though we weren't sure whether or not it was one of those tall tales people tell when they have nothing better to do. People said that Etxepare never used a tape measure, and that to judge the dimensions of a space or a piece of wood, he would just look at it for a while, muse, take off his beret, throw it up in the air, and then toss it to what would be about the right length, not even bothering to measure the width. Just looking carefully was enough. But only those who had been lucky enough to order a piece of furniture from him or to see him, by chance, measuring in the workshop knew for certain if this story was true.

That's why we were so excited when, finally, after a week, Etxepare knocked on our door early one morning. I opened the door, and he looked at me cordially; I stood aside, and he came in. He and grandfather greeted each other, then my mother and father said hello, and then we all went into my parents' bedroom. Etxepare stationed himself in the middle of the room and, behind him, in a semicircle, stood grandfather, my father, my mother, and I. The silence was poignant.

After a minute, Etxepare turned slowly, taking in the room. Then he stopped again, pushed back his beret and scratched his head. That where you want it? he asked my mother with a nod. Yes, there, my mother said. Fine. Then he took off his beret and threw it somewhere below the corner where the wall met the ceiling. That high? Yes, about that high, my mother answered. Fine. And, once the beret was back on, he stepped back from the wall a bit and, measuring with his eyes, said, We'll make it this wide. All right, my mother concurred. Agreed then; I'll start this afternoon. Then Etxepare said see you later, and we stood to one side as he went by, bid farewell again at the door, and closed it silently.

Of course, the problem with actually being there at the start of something like that is that you then have no option but to follow it through, step-by-step, until you see it finished. Not because you doubt that the armoire will fit perfectly into the space agreed upon by Etxepare and your mother—that would be absurd—but because you have to learn how to make something that, having been crafted that way, could last, as they said, more than a lifetime. Because if you're not going to witness it, then you might as well go into any old furniture store and buy any old ready-made armoire. So, inevitably, I had to watch. But I also had to go to school and play, and I couldn't spend all day at the workshop door, staring.

That very afternoon, for example, I ran like mad as soon as school got out so I could spend at least half an hour watching Etxepare before going up to our apartment. The following morning, I hung around a few minutes to watch him work and was late for class. I got half an hour's detention at lunchtime as punishment and then, since on my way home I stopped again to watch Etxepare for a minute before going upstairs, I was late for lunch. I didn't mind being scolded and, fortunately, there were no delays on my way back to school because Etxepare had not come back from his lunch break yet, so the workshop was still closed.

But when I left school at five I sat down to watch him saw and, when I finally got home, I was so late that I wasn't allowed to have my after-school snack.

And on it went, more or less like that, for about a week. It was totally impossible to see how Etxepare was making the armoire and be on time for anything—for school, for games, for lunch, for my after-school snack, for dinner, for anything. Impossible. Then I decided that I was simply going to watch everything Etxepare did without worrying about anything else and without letting anyone see me or know where I was.

That decided, I followed the armoire's construction step-by-step, plank-by-plank, nail-after-nail, while, in silence and without ever speaking to me, Etxepare merely looked at me every once in a while and smiled. I smiled at him, too, and, after a brief pause, we would each go back to our business. That is, he to his work and me to watching his every move: how—with no tape measure—he penciled a line onto the wood; how he sawed; the way he stretched his arm when he used the plane and the shavings fell to the ground; the gentle force with which he used his carpenter's brace; how he sanded and then softly stroked the wood during thoughtful pauses. Me and him, hour after hour, day after day, with no one to disturb us.

Until one night, when the only thing left to do was varnish the armoire, and when in the distance you could hear bombs and the noise of people running through the streets, I got out of bed, opened and closed the front door carefully, walked downstairs, went into the workshop and climbed inside the armoire. Once in, curled up, I hugged myself tighter and tighter in the darkness, and I think I fell asleep.

Years later, after a long silence, I heard voices again, woke up, and ventured out of the armoire. The workshop, once full of golden wood shavings, was a huge field of flowers. The voices I had heard came from a mountain sown with graves. I thought it must be late and that I ought to get home. I began walking along the estuary, as if in a dream, and I came to a demolished street in a demolished town. I found a beret in the rubble and I stopped to listen. And then, finally, Etxepare spoke to me, and he said: It was here. We'll put the armoire here. And now you know it's true; if you measure carefully, anything you make can last more than a lifetime.

Translated by Lisa Dillman

Flesh Sunday

Javier Marías

WE WERE STAYING in the Hotel de Londres and, during our first twenty-four hours in the city we hadn't left our room, we had merely been out onto the terrace to look at La Concha beach, far too crowded for the spectacle to be a pleasant one. An indistinguishable mass is never a pleasing sight, and it was impossible there to fix on anyone, even with binoculars, an excess of bare flesh has a distinctly leveling effect. We had taken the binoculars with us just in case, one Sunday, we went to Lasarte, to the races, there's not much to do in San Sebastián on a Sunday in August, we would be there for three weeks on our holidays, four Sundays but only three weeks, because that second day of our stay was a Sunday and we would be leaving on a Monday.

I spent more time out on the terrace than did my wife, Luisa, always with my binoculars in my hand, or rather,

JAVIER MARÍAS *(Madrid, 1951–) has won many awards for his fiction including the Nelly Sachs Prize and the International IMPAC Dublin Literary Award, as well as the Spanish National Translation Prize for his translation of Tristram Shandy. "Flesh Sunday" is from the collection* When I Was Mortal *(Harvill Press, 1999).*

hanging round my neck so that they didn't slip from my grasp and fall from the terrace to shatter on the ground below. I tried to focus on someone on the beach, to pick someone out, but there were too many people to be able to remain faithful to anyone in particular, I panned across the beach with the binoculars, I saw hundreds of children, dozens of fat men, scores of girls (none of them topless, that's still fairly rare in San Sebastián), young flesh, mature flesh and old flesh, children's flesh, which is not yet flesh, and mother's flesh, which is somehow more fleshy for having already reproduced itself. I soon grew tired of looking and went back to the bed where Luisa was lying down, I kissed her a few times, then returned to the terrace, and again peered through the binoculars. Perhaps I was bored, which is why I felt slightly envious when I saw that two rooms down to my right there was a man, also armed with binoculars, who had them trained on one particular spot, lowering them only from time to time and not moving them at all when he was looking through them: he held them up high, motionless, for a couple of minutes, then he would rest his arm and, shortly afterward, he would raise it again, always in the same position, he didn't change the direction of his gaze one inch. He wasn't leaning out, though, he was watching from inside his room, and so I could only see one hairy arm, now where exactly was he looking, I wondered enviously, I wanted to fix my gaze on something too, it's only when you rest your gaze on something that you really relax and become interested in what you're looking at, I merely made random sweeps, just flesh and yet more indistinguishable flesh, if, when we finally left the room, Luisa and I went down to the beach (we were

According to my calculations and observations, the man to my right had to be looking at one of four people, all fairly close together and lined up in the back row, far from the water's edge. To the right of these people was a small empty space, to their left as well, which was what made me think that he was looking at one of those four. The first person (from left to right, as they say in photo captions) had her face turned to me or us, for she was sunbathing lying on her back: a youngish woman, she was reading a newspaper, she had the top part of her bikini undone, but hadn't removed it entirely (that's still rather frowned upon in San Sebastián). The second person was sitting down, she was older, plumper, wearing a one-piece bathing suit and a straw hat, she was smearing suncream on herself: she must be a mother, but her children were nowhere to be seen, perhaps they were playing by the sea. The third person was a man, possibly her husband or her brother, he was thinner, he was pretending to shiver as he stood on his towel, as if he had just emerged from the sea (he must have been pretending to shiver because the sea would certainly not be cold). The fourth person was the easiest to make out because he was wearing clothes, at least his top half was covered: he was an older man (the hair at the nape of his neck was gray) sitting with his back to us, erect, as if he, in turn, were watching or surveying someone on the shore or some rows ahead, the beach his theater. I fixed my gaze on him: he was evidently alone, he had nothing to do with the man to his left, the man who was pretending to shiver. He was wearing a short-sleeved, green T-shirt, you couldn't see if he had swimming trunks on or trousers, if he was fully dressed, most inappropriate on a beach, if he was, that would cer-

At the Beach

Julián Ayesta

IN THE LATE AFTERNOONS, the beach was full of orange sun and there were lots of white clouds and everything smelled of potato and onion omelette.

And there were crabs that hid among the rocks, and we children were in charge of burying the bottles of cider in the damp sand to keep them cool.

And everyone said, "What a glorious afternoon," and the young couples sat apart from everyone else, and when it began to grow dark and everything was lilac and purple, they would sit very silently with their faces pressed close, as if they were in confession.

JULIÁN AYESTA *(Gijón, Asturias, 1919–96) joined the fascist Falange in 1937 because it was "anti-government, anti-clerical, and pro-European." After the defeat of the Second Republic, he entered the diplomatic service but received poor postings because he participated in critical meetings of the Club Tiempo Nuevo with dissident thinkers Ramón Tamames, Enrique Múgica, and Dionisio Ridruejo. He wrote one novel,* Helena o el mar del verano *(1952), published with the support of Nobel Prize–winning poet Vicente Aleixandre, and a number of short stories. His prose deals with the passage from childhood to adolescence against a backdrop of the Asturian resort city of Gijón and its beaches. A collection of his stories was republished in 2001.*

But the best part was the late-afternoon swim, when the sun was going down and was huge and kept getting redder and redder, and the sea was first green, then a darker green, then blue, then indigo, and then almost black. And the water was so warm, and there were shoals of tiny fishes swimming in and out among the reddish seaweed.

And it was fun diving down and pinching the women on their legs to make them squeal. And then Papa and Uncle Arturo and Aunt Josefina's husband would lift us up onto their shoulders and let us dive into the water. And then two of them would pick one of us up and hurl us through the air, saying, "In he goes, squirming like a cat!" and the women, their bottoms bulging in their antediluvian costumes, would say, "Stop messing around with the kids." And then the men would say to us: "Come on, let's give them a fright," and we would chase Mama and our aunts and the other ladies, and they would scuttle screaming out of the water and up the beach until we caught them and dragged them back, captive, to the water's edge, and there they would sit on the sand, terrified, and Aunt Honorina, close to tears, would say to her husband, "No, please, Arturín, no." And we kids would kill ourselves laughing when she called Uncle Arturo "Arturín," and for at least an hour afterward, until we got tired, we would all call him "Arturín." But then we would join hands (the women's hands would be shaking) and run to the water together and plunge in, not the ladies though—they would sit down where the water was only about two inches deep, laughing like a lot of broody hens. And stupid Albertito would always open his mouth and gulp down lots of water and sand and then vomit it up and be left with a bitter burning sensation inside.

And it was so funny to see Aunt Josefina's legs under the

water—they seemed to swell and shrink and were the same disgusting greenish white as a toad's belly.

And there was an older girl who had just arrived from Madrid, very pretty and very tanned, with really big eyes and smelling of a perfume that made you feel all funny.

And she had a very clear, sad sort of voice, and she used to say to us boys, "Which one of you is brave enough to swim with me out to the Camello," but no one ever dared, not Papa, not Uncle Arturo, not Aunt Josefina's husband, not us, and then she would swim all alone out to the Camello, which was so far off you could hardly see it, and she didn't care if the sea was rough or if it was one of those gray days when you felt afraid even to go in the water. And she swam wearing the bracelets that she always wore, and we would watch as one arm then the other emerged shining and wet, with the sun glinting on her bracelets, and because she was swimming crawl, her feet left behind them a wake of foam.

And there was a bald German gentleman, who wore white bathing trunks and always had two dogs with him, and his skin was burned red, almost black, from spending all day in the sun, fishing and reading the newspaper, with a white towel over his shoulders. And then we would have our afternoon snack on the beach, and for the children there were the lunchtime leftovers—tuna, omelette, and cutlets fried in breadcrumbs, and for dessert we had a choice of oranges, apples, pears, grapes, cherries, or peaches. And there were bananas, too, and we used to have fun squeezing them at one end so that the flesh popped out the other and then showing them to the grownups; it always made the men laugh, though we never knew why.

And the slices of omelette and the cutlets were all gritty with sand, and the little girls' wet hair stuck to their faces, and their eyes shone, and they would scream and leap about among the dogs, who would leap about too and bark and run to fetch the bits of dry seaweed that were thrown for them, and then the girls would give them any scraps, and there was always loads left over—omelette, cutlets, tuna—and the dogs would lick the empty sardine tins until the tins shone like mirrors, and King would even eat the peel from the fruit, although he was the only dog that did.

And because the men said that we mustn't leave a scrap of paper or any rubbish on the beach "because we had to set a good example," we would pile up the cardboard trays and the bits of greasy paper and the peel and set fire to it all and then bury the ashes along with the cans that wouldn't burn.

And then we would go and get dressed behind the rocks. And the sand was really cold, and a cold wind came whipping through, making us shiver because, by then, it was growing dark.

And then everyone—apart from the ladies—would pick up a bag and we would set off home. And we would walk along singing and picking blackberries, which were still warm from the sun.

And our backs were all sticky and stinging, and a great fat moon would be coming up.

And the frogs and the toads would be singing too.

And everything smelled of thyme.

And then we would have to go past the ciderhouses and the bars, which were full of men drinking and playing skittles and pitch-and-toss.

And it was good to hear the sound of wood on wood or the clink of metal on metal.

And there was a man who sang really well, and Papa said why didn't we sit down at one of the tables and rest a while, and he ordered cider for everyone, including the children, and it tickled and bubbled as it went down.

And that was when the stars would come out.

And from time to time, you'd notice a very dark patch of sea, so dark that just the thought of swimming there all alone made you feel afraid.

And Papa and Uncle Arturo asked Aunt Josefina to sing "I've got three little goats," but she turned bright red and said how could she possibly sing in front of all those people, and everyone laughed.

And suddenly a man came over, stinking of wine, and he clapped my father on the back and said something I couldn't hear.

And Papa gave him a nasty look, then immediately paid the bill, and we left.

You could hear music coming from a Sunday dance somewhere.

And by the time we reached Gijón, we were all very quiet, almost sad.

And the lights in the streets were sad too.

And on the beach, you could see the yacht club hung with colored lights.

And there were lots of people in the street, and a band marched past, playing.

And cars with white wheels went by.

And the streets were all newly washed and shining and black.

And everything smelled of hot tires and cologne and sea.

All because the Prince of Asturias was visiting Gijón.

Translated by Margaret Jull Costa

Sibila

Xosé Luís Méndez Ferrín

NOW THAT, BENT BENEATH the burden of the clouded years, I have found the ring again, in front of the house with the triangle (5 Rúa dos Loureiros, Santiago de Compostela) and I know I am going to be visited by Sibila, I recall the gangling figure of the unforgettable Domingos Areal as it looms toward me out of oblivion. And it had all begun when we left the cinema (we had gone to see *Metropolis*) and later met up again for dinner in the Asesino Restaurant, on a cold, frosty night in 1925. Concha had been embarrassed by the glances thrown at her by Otero Espasandín and by the bold, merry tomfoolery of the revelers, aroused by glistening Ulla wine and enormous glasses of anonymous brandy. I remember every detail of that day that was to be rendered horrible

XOSÉ LUÍS MÉNDEZ FERRÍN *(1938–), poet and story-teller, editor and critic, is also a radical Galician nationalist and political thinker. One of the founders of the Unión do Pobo Galego, he served several terms in prison for his outspoken opposition to Franco's repression. This story is taken from* Them and Other Stories *(1996), stories collected from throughout Ferrín's long career, from his first collection published in 1958 to* Arraianos *published in 1991.*

and ever-present within me by the events that followed.
García-Sabell had an examination the next morning, and
he strode off home to Rúa de Xelmírez; Maside, erect as a
birch tree, disappeared into the cold; Xesús Bal decided to
go and see the processions in the Praza da Quintana and,
a solitary figure, he waved good-bye and walked away
whistling "The Firebird." We were left alone, Domingos
Areal and this man who is sitting here now writing this
account with his heart lodged in his throat. We walked in
no particular direction, swathed in our overcoats, our hats
pulled down over our heads, puffing proudly on our pipes:
Rúa do Medio, castellated around by important chim-
neys; Rúa de Bonaval, like a transit to the gray ash and the
dense wretchedness wafted out of each door and window;
the fields of Belvís, taking on frost and an opaque, melan-
choly-laden silence; Rúa dos Lagartos, a street unrivaled
for timidity. A dog barked on the outskirts of the slums of
Compostela as we headed back toward the relief of the
city, with its shields of stone and its streets of slate, talking about nationalism, Manoel Antonio, maybe about
Huidobro. We were free, the city was ours; we were discovering secret alleyways and lighted windows that fired
our youthful imaginations, so irretrievable, now so irretrievable. As I write this account, hardly lifting my pen
from the paper, I am burdened with anguish and foreboding, oppressed by the emotions of times gone by: that ar-
rogant insurrection that we bore in our eyes. Anything
could happen that night because the presence of those
towers, rising in clear outline against a pitter-patter of
stars that wounded our eyes, made our saliva seethe with
the unformed awareness of something absolutely new

lying in wait for us. "There's going to be a cosmic sign. We had better be prepared," Domingos Areal muttered, without removing his pipe from his mouth. He was in secret contact with Krisnamurti, with Roso de Luna, with Vicente Risco. Like Amado Carballo and other sad youths who flitted through this life, he could hear the ethereal call of oriental perfectionism and other celebrated, despicable chimeras that I shall not specify here because I am on the brink of disaster and of the definitive loss of my own being. And it is now that I wish to record, to make a clear statement of the initial fact that caused everything else, as well as my present despair. We were in Rúa dos Loureiros; we were looking at a beautiful house (number 5) the upper story of which consisted of a triangular stone pediment that captured my cubist attention and appealed to Domingos Areal's theosophic curiosity. A flash of lightning—or else some ineffable presence— forced us both to look down at the ground. *And there was the ring, shining like the morning star.* We both pounced. Domingos beat me to it and, with one swift movement, he placed it on the little finger of his left hand, I remember it clearly. He extended his long, hard hand, and we looked at the ring by the light of a street lamp. It displayed a symbol that resembled an ellipse; both of us felt that we were in the presence of mystery. "It has something to do with the triangle on that house," suggested Domingos. I replied: "The ellipse and the triangle do not merely imply contrasting visions of the world, but different conceptual dimensions. That is to say: different ideal spheres." He was not satisfied, and insisted: "It is precisely because of what you say that I assert that the ring and the triangle are related. Read Frazer." I became somewhat annoyed at this and, after disdainfully explaining to him that in the *Golden Bough* (which Fermín Bouza had lent me at the Seminar of Galician Studies) there is no reference to any such relationship, I withdrew into a prickly silence as I contemplated, with decided envy, the lovely ring on my friend's hand. What a magnificent prologue to such a vast, vertiginous tragedy of death and beauty! Now, before pausing in the writing of my account to contemplate, with infinite nostalgia and infinite grief, the portrait of Domingos Areal (drawn by Maside, that same year of 1925, on the check tablecloth on that same round table in the Asesino Restaurant where this story begins amid an inaudible clattering of metal), I wish to manifest my belief that terror and violence, when they acquire the support of aesthetically valid formulae, multiply their infamy and their denial of basic human dignity. As I say this, the dark eyes of the difficult and dour poet and artist Domingos Areal appear before me, witnesses to the roots of wretchedness, and lost now forever. Maside had given him lips with bitter lines, the lips he gave everyone, yet the form of the cravat softened the whole, otherwise rigid and full of foreboding. It is possible that those persons for whom this account is intended will not fully understand what follows—and the blame must lie with me—yet what is certain is that the private life of the man who is writing it was left divided in two that night, as when a pear is cut in half. And, on this side of the divide in my existence, I recall meetings with Domingos Areal: at a reserved table in the Café Suízo, each of us puffing away at a Havana cigar generously provided by Filgueira

Valverde's father, while a horripilation of vile flamenco
music echoed around us and cabaret fumes assaulted our
eyes in a fury of raging colors; in the churchyard in Rúa da
Quinta Angustia, listening to a distant clock strike two in
the morning, as fog silenced the city and even invaded our
valiant avant-garde hearts; in a sordid cafe on Rúa Travesa, with the boundless background of the thousand
voices of the market bringing us the voices of the peasant
and the peddler, invading the strip of traders that starts at
San Fiz de Solovio Church and ends at the Porta do
Camiño; in Rúa da Caramoniña, displaying its navel-
worts (or perhaps hemlock) lodged in those crevices in
the wall that offered spongy, secret, romantic shelter. On
each occasion the ring, with its ellipse, was shining on
Domingos Areal's finger, and pallor was clouding his
cheeks, violet was invading the rings under his eyes of
trembling jet, the burden of something abominable was
bowing his shoulders with a cruel diligence, intermittent
earthquakes muddled his words, and his aching teeth
clattered like a jazz band as his saliva spurted into my
face, the long-suffering face of a faithful friend. He was in
rapid decline; wasting away; he no longer frequented the
cafe or the promenade; he sought me out as a confidant.
How he was rushing toward his end! (Now that the death
of the present writer is imminent, that other death, my
friends, will finally be revealed, a warning and a threat to
all of you who are reading this.) Because the fact is—take
careful note of what follows—that from the moment
Domingos Areal took possession of the ring with the ellipse, in front of the house with the triangle in Rúa dos
Loureiros, *a bewitching person appeared before him in his*

dreams each night. A woman without equal, I remember
Domingos's voice precisely, muffled by the books in the
university library, when, tormented by anxiety, he seized a
pencil and said: "Look at her." All the silence and the
sweet smell of a dusty past were captured in the sketch
that he drew on the notepad before me. Castelao had
always been warm in his praise of the tormented lines of
Domingos Areal's Mattissian sketches, a counterpoint to
the excesses of Cándido Fernández Mazas and other
audacious Francophiles of the past, who had been encour-
aged by the butterfly words of that man Rafael Dieste.
But this was different: from the squares on the paper there
emanated a powerful woman's face, softly strong (like the
baroque cylinders on the Convent of Santa Clara, seen
against the light, at sunset on certain days), balmy, with
sweet, frightened eyes like meadows, or like crystal
streams running through beech groves that are never
wounded by the sun; with fleshy lips that betrayed some
childish, velvety fear, a look of universal perplexity. "It's
the Delphic Sibyl!" I cried instantly. Because nothing
could have been more like that figure immortalized by
Michelangelo in the Sistine Chapel. Domingos looked at
the paper with infinite surprise. "Maybe she came to
Michelangelo in dreams as well," he practically shouted,
and Bustamante the librarian, who was passing by, his
innkeeper's overall sweeping the floor, demanded absolute
silence, thrusting his Unamunian chin into our faces. Because every night Sibila came, came to him. And now I
warn you, the addressees of this text, that there are no
words with which to bring to my narration the con-
fidences of my unfortunate friend. She had appeared in

the center of his dreams, preceded by an immense triangle
and enclosed in an elliptic line, ever since the moment he
discovered the ring in Rúa dos Loureiros and put it on his
finger. What at first had been a happy, astonishing surprise (as he told me in the Café Suízo), turned, night by
night, into a sackful of lead. I had not yet read Freud, perhaps due to certain suspicions expressed by the timid Rof
Carballo (a great admirer of Claudel). All that I knew—
about dreams—was Carlos Maside's bold, interpretive
ramblings, frivolously combined with white coffee in the
Café Español. She (we had called her Sibila ever since
discovering the similarity in the university library) would
come wrapped in heavy clothing, motionless and dyna-
mic, and from each triangular piece of her robe there
would emerge a soft, musical ellipse that filled Domingos's dream with a palpitating aroma of a swallow or any
other slight, fluttering creature. She would draw him to
her breast and delirium would follow in sweet and extra-
ordinarily destructive copulation. He felt drained, more
and more defeated day by day. Domingos's language could
not accommodate such a wealth of pleasure and beauty, of
sound and clashing of colors and messages of light and
the progressive loss of his own being (he said this in Rúa
da Quinta Angustia). Domingos had almost reached the
point of neither eating nor smoking by the night that
Sibila, resplendent, arrived clutching an automatic pistol,
with a cruel look instead of lips. She had sat in a large
metal chair (the Bauhaus type, you know the sort) and *the
ellipses had disappeared,* or had been rubbed off, or had
been extinguished, which horrified my friend perhaps because of some secret intuition related to his theosophic

beliefs. Sibila had sat there and had stared at my friend with eyes of steel and with all the evil in the world, until dawn and the sound of bells came to rescue him for wakefulness and for light—if there was now any rescuing him. He told me all this in the little café on Rúa Travesa, and he added in horror: "She had a blue swastika tattooed on her forehead." It seems that this was when Domingos began his last race toward degradation and destruction, and everything that he told me, after our meeting in Rúa da Caramoniña, was charged with horrible vagueness. In each dream Domingos performed rites of humiliation before Sibila while irresolute flageolets and organs sounded, and an abominable, wet substance flowed like pus from her mouth as she sat there—as she sat there on a bamboo throne, naked, her whole body tattooed with triangles. The terrible swastika would now always preside on her forehead, as clear as a November moon, and the ellipses had disappeared. For the suppression of the ellipse-triangle coupling and its replacement by the swastika-triangle coupling I can find no noble interpretation, because everything leads me to a deep belief in the fatal establishment of an *until then unsuspected order of cruelty and beauty.* As night fell over Compostela, I would think of my friend, and I felt for him. In the absolute solitude of his garret, as soon as he fell asleep, Sibila would enter his dreams. And because I knew how these sessions of torture were developing, I suffered for my suffering friend. Sibila subjected him to nefarious treatment: the insertion of stilettos into unutterable places, the chewing of vermicular objects, practices with his own excrement and that of others. "Everything always culminates in perfect ecstasy.

The Confession

Manuel Rivas

WHAT DO YOU SAY? What do you say to a boy when he presses up close to you?

I tell him not to get so close.

What if you like him, though? Do you let him get a bit closer?

Yes, a bit.

What do you mean by a bit. A lot?

No, not a lot!

And when you let him get that little bit closer . . .

But I don't!

You said you did.

Only a little. Only a very little bit closer.

You must never lie in confession. Remember you are talking to God. Tell God the truth! You'll feel better after-

MANUEL RIVAS *(A Coruña, 1957–) is a journalist and writer. He writes in Galician and translates his own work into Spanish. He won the national Critics Prize for the novel* The Carpenter's Pencil, *and his story "The Butterfly's Tongue" has been made into a successful film. "The Confession" is from his most recent collection of short stories,* As chamadas perdidas.

ward, cleansed! Now tell me: when you let him get that little bit closer, can you feel his body?

His body? No, not his body!

Can't you feel his arms?

Yes, I can feel his arms.

His shoulders?

Yes, his shoulders too.

His legs?

Sometimes.

When the music is very slow, can you feel his knee trying to push in between your legs?

I never let him push very far.

How far?

Like I said, just a little bit.

And his hands. Where does he put his hands?

It's a dance for couples.

Yes, but where exactly does he put his hands?

On my waist.

But where on your waist?

Where else? On my midriff, like I said, on my waist.

Yes, but above or below?

Around my middle.

And he doesn't move it lower? Doesn't he sometimes move his hand lower?

Sometimes he moves it lower, sometimes higher.

And you let him move it lower and higher?

A little. Just to change position slightly. But I'd never let him go too far.

What do you do if he does?

I put the brakes on.

How do you do that?

I stiffen up!

But if he insists, and you really like him, don't you give in? Don't you surrender?

No, Father. I'm tempted, but I resist.

Don't you let yourself go, even for a moment?

Possibly. For a moment, yes.

And what do you feel then?

His heart.

Are you sure you don't feel anything else?

No, just his heart.

And what does his heart do?

It thumps.

It thumps?

Yes, it thumps.

Tell me one last thing. If, when you put the brakes on, he continues, you know, if he perseveres, then what do you do?

I tell him to keep his paws to himself!

But what do you actually say to him, child?

Paws off!

Oh, please, please, say that again!

Paws off!

She had had fun at the seamstresses' house. When she told them about the confession, they laughed so much the tears rolled down their cheeks.

SEAMSTRESS 1: Poor man! He's fallen in love with you, Marisa!

SEAMSTRESS 2: In love? If you ask me, that new priest is a bit of a lecher!

SEAMSTRESS 1: No, he's just fed up with all the prim old

ladies. When he gets the chance to confess a young girl, he doesn't want to let her go.

SEAMSTRESS 2: Why didn't you just tell him where to go?

I did think about it, said Marisa. But then . . . I don't know. It was like playing some kind of word game with him.

Shortly after she left their house, night descended upon her. She remembered the old riddle: The more there is of me the less you can see. Who am I? Me! replied the darkness with its great toothless mouth. Not that she could get lost. It was the path itself —cut between steep embankments—that led her on, her feet guided by the ruts left by the carts. She wasn't easily scared. On the contrary, she found a kind of comfort in the night, as she did in solitude. It was the silence, the thick silence, that put her on the alert. On certain sleepless nights in her childhood, in order to walk about in the attic without being heard and to avoid the treacherous creak of the wooden floorboards, she used to hold her breath and almost levitate across the floor in her woollen socks. It was that kind of presence she sensed watching her now, keeping pace with her, behind the overhang of scrub, along the top of the embankment. A way of walking without touching the ground, cushioned with dead leaves. Suddenly she felt very weak. Her body did not respond to the orders from her brain. The more quickly she tried to walk, the more her legs resisted, simultaneously stiff and unsteady. She tried to say an Our Father to free herself from those invisible bonds, but the chain holding her body in check also prevented her from speaking.

There had been no sightings of the wolf for a long time. Sometimes people came across dismembered, half-eaten remains. But some said that, judging from the bite marks, the wounds were inflicted not by a wolf, but by dogs abandoned by hunters and people in the town, dogs who had lost their slavish nature and now attacked in wild packs. Her father, though, had actually come face to face with the wolf. That is why the wolf had entered her world not as a legend from the remote past, but as an inheritance that still howled along the outermost frontiers of her memory. But fear, real fear, her father had told her, comes not from seeing the wolf. Fear disappears when you have the wolf there before you. Real fear, paralyzing fear, comes when you sense that the wolf is near.

She did not have a stick handy nor did she want to go looking for one. She had no lighter, no matches, nothing with which she could make a noise. The mere thought of crouching down to pick up a stone made her feel dizzy. This is what people mean when they speak of being frozen by fear. The kind of fear that creates more fear. The idea that any movement, either in flight or in self-defense, will be turned to your disadvantage. The flow of her voice, the one weapon she could trust, had stopped at the dam formed by her throat and turned around and was, instead, purring inside her intestines, as if the words had grown fat with anxiety. When she thought about it, though, the voice can do marvelous things. Hers had served her very well. She wasn't given to sudden impulses and was humble in her desires, but whenever she expressed them, they almost always came to pass. When a shooting star crossed the sky—such stars were souls on their way to heaven—you had to say: May God guide you, and then immediately make a wish. You had to make the wish in secret and keep it to yourself. One day, her little sister, a bit of a daydreamer and as happy as a lark, had announced to the family that she had seen a shooting star from the balcony before she went to bed. There was no need to ask what she had wished for—she was quick to reveal it herself: I asked to join Manolita Chen's Chinese Theater and to go away with them. It was suppertime and no one said a word, all of them with their heads down, staring into their soup bowls, as if hoping to find the trail left by a star that had fallen into the sea.

And then, her little sister went on—pleased at having captured everyone's attention so successfully that she had provoked not only her family's silent concern, but also the crackling of the fire in the hearth and the noisy curiosity of the wind rousing the windows with the bare knuckles of branches—and then, she went on, I dreamed that when I was in the field tending the cows, Manolita Chen turned up wearing a blue silk dress and a big white hat and she said: Come along, child, come with me! You're much too pretty to be a servant of cows and a governess of chickens.

Everyone burst out laughing, but the sternest of her brothers asked: Who taught you a fancy expression like that?

What fancy expression?

The one about you being a governess of chickens.

Xan das Bolas, the one in the movies, he taught me to say that!

You mean you've seen Xan das Bolas around here as well?

Yes, the same day I saw Manolita Chen.

Aren't you the lucky one! The inside of your head must be one nonstop cabaret.

From now on, said their father very gravely, with all the solemnity of the irrefutable, and looking around at his other children, from now on, she will no longer tend the cattle or do heavy work or clean out the chickens. She will help in the house and study, and that's all.

The word, like the shooting star, can be quite powerful.

Out of that family portrait, Marisa heard two voices speak to her.

Look fear straight in the eye, her father was saying. She looked. But fear did not return her gaze. All she saw was a vast expanse of dense shadow. The whole forest resembled some fabulous, demented creature.

The other voice was that of her little sister. She was laughing at her and saying: Make the sign of the cross!

If she could manage to bring her thumb up to the middle of her forehead, it would be easy, because when you make the sign of the cross on your body, you do so downward. She hurriedly crossed herself, reciting the formula in a mechanical mumble.

> By the sign
> of the Holy Cross
> deliver us from our enemies, O Lord
> our God
> in the name of the Father
> and the Son
> and the Holy Ghost
> Amen.

No, no, not like that, said her little sister, laughing. Repeat after me, slowly and fearlessly:

By the sign
of the Holy Toast
I ate some pork
as dry as chalk
the more they gave
the more I craved
to punish him
for what he'd done
I took some rope
to tie him up
and heard him sing:
To hell with you
and your piece of string.

In proud, alchemical splendor, the moon emerged from
between the tall laurel hedges. Startled by this sudden brilliance, the rogue stumbled, and Marisa heard the sound of
a dry twig snapping, shattering that atmosphere of dense
fear. Liberated, she clambered boldly up the steep slope to
peer over the top. Silhouetted against the hillside she saw
the fleeing, cassocked figure of the father confessor.

Translated by Margaret Jull Costa

Amnesia

Germán Sierra

SO I SAY GOOD MORNING and the woman behind the counter says good morning and I say, excuse me, I need some help, I need to know if I was here earlier, about three hours ago, and, taking cover behind the cheeses and mortadella and sausages and smoked salmon, she looks at me like I'm crazy and I say, if I was here, I probably bought mortadella because I really like mortadella, you know? And she backs up and doesn't answer and keeps looking at me suspiciously and I say, can you make me a mortadella sandwich?, maybe that way I'll remember if I ate one earlier on; sure, all right, she says. You'll have to excuse me, you must think I'm crazy; I'm sick but not

GERMÁN SIERRA *(A Coruña, 1960–) has published short stories, essays, and three novels. The most recent,* Efectos secundarios, *was awarded the Jaén Prize in 2000. Currently working as a neuroscientist at the University of Santiago de Compostela, he writes literary pieces that deal with the reciprocal interference between science and contemporary fiction. "Amnesia" depicts a fast-talking narrator who claims to have forgotten what happened to a chunk of his morning and stops off on the way to Santiago de Compostela to solicit help in a roadside bar.*

crazy, I just had an amnesia attack. Memory loss, you know, you must have seen it in the movies, when someone gets hit on the head and loses their memory? Well, that's post-traumatic amnesia, though that's not my problem, since I didn't bang my head. My problem is very unusual. The doctors are stumped. Generally, you lose your memory if you've been unconscious. But in my case it's like an attack. Suddenly—bam!—everything gets erased. Like it never happened. Whole hours at a time. Like I've leapt through time and all that time just vanished. Like I've been asleep, though I know I haven't been unconscious, I know because it's happened in front of other people before and they told me and told my doctor that I acted normal right up to the moment—bam—when the preceding hours just get erased, and it feels like I've leapt through time instantaneously. It's very very strange, as you can imagine.

She looks at me with that respect that older women show toward illness. More than fear or compassion, it's a pantheistic reverence for the forces of nature, like what you feel when you see a storm over the ocean or a volcano eruption.

It doesn't happen often, I continue, but when it does it's really inconvenient. It's not that the forgetting itself is inconvenient; forgetting is necessary—my doctor says that forgetting is part of learning, that if we didn't forget the trivial aspects of our feelings we wouldn't be able to remember the important things. But unfortunately, when it happens to me, I forget everything, it's like that time never existed; but it did exist, I spoke to people, and I did things, so my past exists in other people's memories, which proves that it was also part of me. Memory is a strange phenomenon—we always think it's ours that matters, and we go crazy when we forget things. Don't you forget things? But really, our memory is never entirely our own, nothing is entirely our own, even memory is a dialogue, several memories communicating with each other. We accept other people's memories as if they were our own more often than we think.

Can you see my predicament? Three hours ago I was passing through, or at least I think I was, I think I was passing through because I remember I'd planned to stop in here. Well, strictly speaking, what I know for sure is that an hour ago I was in Santiago, and what it feels like to me is that I just turned up there, suddenly, like I'd been beamed in, you know, like in those science fiction movies where someone gets vaporized by a ray-gun, disappears, and then reappears on another planet. Because all I remember is that the split second before that I was at home, a hundred kilometers away, right?, needing to go to Santiago, and suddenly, like magic, I turn up in Santiago. What I can remember, perfectly, is what I was planning to do while I was at home: I had to take a blue packet with important information in it to Santiago. The thing is, I don't even know what the information is. And then there I was, in Santiago, in the middle of the street, with no blue packet. I lost the packet and I lost my memory. And when you lose something, what you do is you retrace your steps to go back the way you came and try to find it. But I lost the packet and I lost my way. So now I'm trying to find the way to find the packet.

It's not like this happens to me a lot; if it did I could never do anything. It's not the first time, but in the last five years it's only happened three or four times. The doctor calls them episodes, like on a TV series. So, in my previous episodes I wasn't doing anything important; see, what's dangerous about this is that something really important might have happened and you'd never know, you might have won the lottery, or met someone really special—because I'm single, you know—and never know that you made a date with her. Or like now, this is important, I have to get that packet back and into the hands of whoever it's addressed to, and that's why I need to know if I was here before. I think I might have stopped here because I've come before, you might not remember me from before, but I stop in for your mortadella. I like mortadella and it's hard to find the good kind, and today, before I left, I planned to stop at your store, which is why I've come now, to see if I came in before.

The woman says she's almost sure I didn't stop in earlier, she's been behind the counter almost all day, and when she went out she left her daughter in charge. Her daughter is in the kitchen; she calls her. Her daughter is a smiling young woman, a little on the pudgy side, about twenty, twenty-two years old, wearing an apron over her jeans. Her daughter hasn't seen me today, either. She remembers seeing me on other occasions, maybe a month ago. And before that. She remembers that a month ago I sat at one of the tables in the bar area to have a sandwich and a beer. But not today. They both decide that I haven't been in today. Bad start. The mother explains my problem to the daughter. Poor man, losing his memory like that, at least he only forgot a couple of hours, that's not too long, though I can think of plenty of places where he might have stopped along the way. The daughter asks me if I'm sure I didn't already deliver the packet and I say yes, I'm sure, I've already asked if they got it; she asks if I've looked in the car. My car is parked outside the store and I've already searched it top to bottom, twice. Let's go look again. I'll help you. But have a coffee first; sit down at one of the tables and rest for a minute, poor man. In one corner, sitting by a window that looks out over the road and through which I can see my car, a deadpan grandfather presides over the scene. The mother makes coffee for both of us while the daughter takes me to a table, says she'll help me find the packet, asks what's in it; and I say I don't know, but they're important papers for my sister that I can't lose. If my illness makes me lose them, my sister could get into some trouble that has nothing to do with her. It's hard to explain. I shouldn't worry, the daughter says, the packet will turn up somewhere. If it were full of money it would be one thing, someone might have just kept it, but if it's just papers, if they're only any good to your sister, if someone finds it they'll probably take it to the town hall, because we don't have a lost and found here, and whenever someone finds something and wants to give it back, they take it to the town hall or the church, so we could go to the church, too, to see, because the priest usually puts a sign on the door saying such and such an object has been found, and will the owner please come and claim it in the vestry. Sometimes even stolen objects turn up, not because the thief repents—if anything he might get a little scared—but normally the civil guard turns it in, and, if the thief is a minor and the son of a well-known member of the community, then, well, they won't arrest him, they'll just give him a good talking-to, tell his parents, and then the boy goes to see the priest and says, Father, I found this. The priest puts the sign up on the church door and everybody's happy, even if later on people find out what really happened. But you can't put a kid in jail for troublemaking, which is all it usually is, because we don't really have any junkies here—we used to, but they've gone to the city now, or died, or given up. What about you? What do you do? I work for a notary, I say. Oh! Are you a lawyer? No, just an employee, not much more than an errand boy, really. It's not easy to get a good job without a degree. When I was younger I wanted to study journalism, but back then you had to go to Madrid or Barcelona. So then I chose philosophy, but I dropped out, because I was too restless for college. I started working, here and there, to earn a living.

The mother brings the coffees and shoots her daughter a warm, though warning, look as she runs her hands through her fake, bleached curls, which I think would have looked better straighter and darker. The mother is still a little wary of me, she's not sure whether or not I am totally crazy, though she seems to approve of her daughter being so chatty with strangers and sitting down to talk to me and trying to console me, talking to me in order to calm me down. I think the first time I spoke to her my tone was too strident and it gave her a start, because I was distraught, very upset, and though I'm still concerned about the blue packet, I'm a little more composed now, and thanks to our little exchange I've managed to forget about my forgetting a little bit and I sip my coffee very slowly, because it's very hot. Older women like coffee boiling hot because they want to warm up their insides but it's always too hot for me; my mouth and tongue are very sensitive to heat. Would you still like that mortadella sandwich? Yes, thank you, I think I should eat something, the search might take a while and I can't remember if I had breakfast or not. When I left, I planned to stop and eat something, and that's why I started looking for where I might have stopped for some food.

Let's go search your car, the daughter says. It's cold out; the mud parking lot is almost frozen. You should put something else on, the mother says, you'll catch cold, and she goes into the kitchen and comes back out with a brown wool coat and puts it over her shoulders. She never covers up! she says. I open the car, carefully search through every one of the papers on the dashboard, the daughter, meanwhile, feels around under the front seats, lifts them up, finds nothing but dirt. The back seat doesn't come up. Kneeling on it, she rummages through the folders on the back window shelf, opens them one by one and shows me their contents. Is this it? No. What about this? No. I open the trunk. Let me do it, you're going to get filthy, I say. There are sticky black grease stains, dirty tools, a banged up cardboard box with a pair of very old shoes in it, a scruffy cap, rags, gum boots. A plastic tackle box. I used to like to go fishing, but I hardly ever do anymore. Sundays I'd go out to the rocks, put on my boots and cap and spend all day trying to lure out conger eels. I almost never caught anything, but I always stayed until the sun went down and at the end of the day I felt like I was bursting with the time I'd spent, just the opposite of how I feel now, after my amnesia attack. The sea stays in your eyes, the salt stays in your mouth and it's nice. I've always liked salty things, like the sea and cheese and mortadella; not candy so much, although I prefer sweet to bitter, which is why I put a lot of sugar in black coffee.

I notice that one of my headlights is broken, the bumper

dented. They weren't like that before, did I have an accident? If so, maybe this time the amnesia was brought on because of a bump on the head. Would I have told my insurance company? If I hit someone, maybe he or she could give me a clue, tell me where I was, what I had done or where I stopped. I always talk a lot, tell people what's going on, though I don't mention my amnesia attacks because they might think I'm crazy. But I can't call the insurance company and ask if I called earlier. What would they think if I said I couldn't remember if I'd had an accident? They'd try to find out if the amnesia was due to the accident and, if they got a hold of my medical records, no one would ever insure me again. It could cause a lot of trouble at the notary office, too. My boss, of course, doesn't know anything about my episodes, one's never happened at work before. If he finds out I'll lose my job, that's for sure, and who would give me a job with a record like this? I don't even know if I could get classified as a cripple and be eligible for disability, because the truth is I'm not a cripple and anyway, I couldn't live off that allowance alone. Fortunately, my neurologist is very discreet. A great doctor, he's successfully treated loads of really tricky cases, but my case is trickier than most. It's even been published, in an American journal, and without using my real name, of course.

The daughter comes with me to the town hall. I tell her it's not necessary, she shouldn't bother, I can find it. But she insists on coming with me and asking me questions and feeling sorry for me. The town hall is housed in a big old building with balconies and flags on the balconies and a security guard at the door who looks like he's about to fall asleep. I'm surprised that it's on such a narrow street, because in general town halls tend to be in squares and have clock towers, which don't work most of the time but somehow symbolize the preeminence of the local council. This building doesn't look very authoritative at all; it's hardly distinguishable from the rest of the buildings on the block.

The daughter speaks to the uniformed guard at the entrance; they're on a first-name basis. She asks him if anyone has turned in a blue packet this morning and he says no, nothing has been handed in all day, but she can go and ask at the church. She thanks him, asks me what time it is; it's just after one. We might find the priest, since mass must be over by now. We don't have to go back for the car since the church is at the end of the same street, in a square as it should be, a real stone square with a fountain in the middle, surrounded by a strip of grass that nobody seems bothered to cut. A lot of women say hi to the daughter while she walks beside me on the narrow sidewalk surrounding the square and then they look at me, curiously, I'd almost even say impertinently. The Romanesque church is four-sided and the parish priest far-sighted. He hasn't received anything today, either, though he does have a message for her mother. I tell the girl I can drop her off at the store, that I have to think about the next place I can go to ask questions. She asks me if the packet's delivery is urgent and I say probably. Otherwise, why send me instead of using a courier or registered mail, like people normally do? She's still interested in figuring out what could be in the packet and speculates it must be something confidential, and I lost it. What a catastrophe! As we walk back to my car she keeps trying to cheer me up, even flirts with me. I have the feeling she doesn't want to go back to the store, that she's trying to use my company as an excuse not to go back to work. In spite of her friendliness, I feel a little uneasy about burdening her with my problems.

She tells me that there are hardly any customers these days, that her mother and the woman she hired have no problem coping. I didn't see any woman, she must be in the kitchen. She tells me that she is, and that since I have to pass by on my way back at any rate, she could go with me on my search, if I don't mind, if I like the idea. She has a brainwave: if I can just remember what happened first thing in the morning, if I tell her everything I remember in chronological order, maybe I will pick up speed and the momentum will make me keep remembering once I get to the part that seems to have vanished, it would be like gathering force, like, she says, when you learn something by heart, like when you're a kid and you learn to recite your times tables and then the teacher asks you what seven times eight is and to remember it you have to start at the beginning of the sevens; when I was in school they called that knowing something by heart, and maybe, impelled by mnemonic force, I could keep remembering, filling the blank space, following my path and the packet's path over the course of the day until I could latch onto it, mentally. As my neurologist would say, it would be like triggering neuron circuits in my brain that must somehow be related once they activated a temporal sequence, letting some neurons set others in motion. I don't remember having tried this before. At least not with any particular aim, with any special effort. And certainly not with an audience. That might be key. A story is different from a chain of recollections, requires extra effort. Even though I can't activate them, I think the images of the packet through time are there, in my head, in a series although I can't conjure them up. I picture trying to trap a cricket, its nest in a field; you can hear it call, crick-et, crick-et, here and there, but you can't tell exactly where it's coming from. When I was a kid I used to catch crickets and put them in little plastic cages and feed them lettuce for days, I think lots of kids used to do that, thirty or forty years ago. I don't think she ever caught crickets, even though she lives so close to the country. It's very hard to tell where sounds come from out in the open; the wind carries them in its gusts and confuses you. My brain takes in these images in gusts, too, and the hours that vanished must be there somewhere, because the doctor says that, even if I can't remember, they are still in there, someplace, sort of warped. Who knows?

She sits beside me in the car. This morning, I tell her as I start the car, I left home very early. I sleep badly in the winter, the taste of darkness wakes me up. The streets were empty, it was foggy and cold. They used to execute the condemned at dawn, that's when people meet their destinies. For me, I say, it's the witching hour, just before day breaks.

My sister called me on my cell phone, I continue. I hate cell phones, but I need one for work. Of course, on the road, in the mountains, all you can hear is screeching and distorted, electronic-sounding voices, like in that German song "Trans Europe Express" from a few years back. She said she was in trouble, she and her boyfriend, that there was a packet at my house, she'd left it there, and I had to deliver it, it was urgent. The thing I can't stand about my sister is not that she's always creating problems but that she's unable to get into trouble on her own account. One of the reasons I left the city, in fact, was to be free of her parties, her sexual problems—I think I'm a lesbian, I think I'm pregnant, you're so rude to my friends. . . .

Sorry, I say, I always ramble. It's even occurred to me that my poor memory might be a result of the fact that I talk too much, as if regaining parts of my memory made something else spill over and I couldn't get it back, though that's probably ridiculous. I make a mental note—the gas station. The bar behind it. That's another place I stop a lot. She tells me not to worry, to keep talking, that she likes listening to me. I get the feeling she is trying to draw out the conversation, well, more like the monologue, with the aim of establishing some sort of trust. She seems enthralled, compelled to listen. She's wearing a slightly grotesque, affectionate expression that seems to indicate that she is really paying attention to me. My neurologist always pays attention to me, something you really appreciate in a doctor. I think good doctors should be able to listen carefully and to explain their diagnoses very precisely. Anyway, I'm not planning on telling you everything I know or can conceive of. I suspect that the packet contains something that could put someone important in a compromising position, documents my sister's boyfriend can use as leverage, so they'll leave him alone. Probably about money or pills. My sister's boyfriend deals, he has a little lab. See, you don't have to be Woodward, Corey, or George Wittig to produce MDMA, DMT, or MDA; any idiot with a recipe and simple instructions can churn out impure Ecstasy. In fact recently, a couple of dealers, pushers, as the press calls them, were arrested with pockets full of colored pills stamped with little playboy bunnies and cartoon characters. In the paper they go on about some imaginary, oafish, tattooed Viking driving into the city in a foreign car, but I know perfectly well from my hairdresser's groupies that my sister's boyfriend is the number one supplier.

Do you remember anything? she asks. Sorry, I say, my mind's on the road, there's so much traffic. I'd love to be driving on an empty highway, through a desert or a plain, getting high on the solitude and the nothingness, like one of those American interstates out west that cross endless plains, cornfields, and deserts. Memory means nothing there, because the landscape never changes. If you get lost, you're lost forever.

I don't take pills, I think, because I'm afraid of getting lost forever, there's an even greater risk with my condition. One night I went with my sister to the Time Machine, that club on the outskirts of town, and I saw a young redhead with a pierced nose and belly button stop dancing in a trance and collapse in time to the music, saw a huge skinhead have tonic convulsions, saw a weekend drag queen vomit all over the DJ. All that popular expressionism is both grotesque and beautiful at the same time. People can choose any type of recreation they want to. It doesn't surprise me that so many people try to prolong their emotions by using chemical substances, because life is running away from them too fast, the way it runs from me when I have an episode. Losing a few memories isn't what matters; what disappears, usually, is the overall significance of memory. The source of that constant beat inside that says: me . . . me . . . me. . . . They try to drug it for one fleeting moment. They try to use the friction that builds up with that series of artificial emotions, kind of like what I'm doing now, reaching out, creating a link with the words flowing from my head and—bam!—my memories, compressed in some remote spot, expand violently, the history of my immediate past emerges from my subconscious and there's the packet, the blue, rectangular envelope. I can see the shock on her face; we almost drive off the road, I stop. About five kilometers away, I calculate, you can see the silhouette of a small town that sprawls out over a gray-green hill. Where the hell is the sea? I could see it off in the distance for ten or fifteen minutes but then it disappeared. I lean back against the seat and light a cigarette, a Marlboro Light. She keeps asking, do you remember? do you remember? Two cars pass us, going more than 200 kilometers an hour and leaving silvery air streams in their wake. I know where the packet is, it's in good hands, I don't even have to go pick it up. It's Saturday, I don't have to work until Monday; she looks at me from the passenger seat.

I'm going to drop you off at home, I say.

She doesn't seem surprised. I think she is mentally ticking off a small success but with a crack to repair, a few broken threads in the web ensnaring us. Come pick me up tonight, we can go for a drink, she says, and it's an irresistible summons, with all the heart and soul she puts in the promise.

Translated by Lisa Dillman

Journey to the Moon

Julio Llamazares

TELEVISION CAME TO OLLEROS IN 1963. The first
one arrived at Martiniano's bar and caused a great stir. On
the day of its debut the whole town turned out. I'd never
seen so many people, not even on payday.

We'd been hearing rumors for several months. In Sabero
there were already two televisions—one in the engineers'
villa and one in the casino—and in Cistierna, three or four.
Those who'd seen one said it was better than the movies
because, for one thing, you could have it at home. José Luis,
from La Herrera, who'd gone to Cistierna with his father
to see it, said it was a radio but you could see the people who
were talking.

JULIO LLAMAZARES *(1955–) was born in the village of
Vegamián, León. The village disappeared beneath the waters of the
Poma reservoir (now drained), and the experience marked him for
life, permeating his writing. He won the Jorge Guillén Prize for
poetry in 1982. His classic novel of vanishing rural Spain,* La lluvia
amarilla *(1988), will be published in English translation in 2003.
This extract is from* Escenas del cine mudo, *a set of evocations of
Spain inspired by a family photo album. He now works as a journalist
and writer in Madrid.*

This pronouncement left me stunned. Although José Luis insisted on it and invoked his father as a witness, which was like invoking God—we weren't about to ask him—I couldn't fathom how you could see someone who was so far away (I'd already accepted you could hear them, though I couldn't fathom that either), and I stared at my own radio hoping one night a miracle would happen. But the miracle didn't happen. The radio went on in its same old accent and kept to its usual routine and, no matter how hard I looked, I couldn't see the people who were talking, despite the fact that more than once I willed myself to picture what their faces might look like. And so, the day Martiniano brought the television, I was one of the first to go to see it, and I saw it, albeit only through the window.

It arrived one Saturday afternoon on the daily bus. Martiniano had gone all the way to León to buy it and he brought it back packed in a box so big that he and the driver could barely lift it down between them. I immediately offered to help. I used to do that sometimes, for a tip, with the shopkeepers who brought packages in on the bus (not just me—lots of other boys did the same thing, which sometimes led to fights and arguments among the contenders), but that day I was willing to help Martiniano for free. I was even ready to pay, provided I could carry the television set. But Martiniano refused my help saying it was very fragile, and I had to be satisfied with following along with all the other people who'd come out to wait for him.

It was, I remember, like a procession. From the bus stop to the bar, which was only about a hundred meters, Martiniano struggled along with the box, surrounded by a swarm of little kids; we didn't take our eyes off that box for a single second. There were also a few grown men coming along behind, passengers who'd come in on the bus or been waiting at the stop and friends of Martiniano's who'd been in the bar and, seeing the bus pull in, come out to wait for him. But he wouldn't let even his friends touch the box. Not them and not his wife. Martiniano was so nervous about his purchase that he didn't want anyone to touch it.

In the bar—where he wouldn't allow us kids, leaving us to watch everything through the window—Martiniano put the box on the floor and, after contemplating it for a few moments, removed his jacket, took a pair of scissors, and began to unpack it. I'll never forget that scene. Huddled at the window with the rest of the kids and even a few women, also eager to see (making for shoves and the odd altercation), I watched Martiniano unpack the box, remove lots of plastic wrapping, and finally take out the television set and place it on a table, handling it more carefully than if it had been a baby. A child certainly never got such a reception in Olleros, where we were legion.

The next day, Sunday, Martiniano gave the television its premiere. The news had flown through the village and, starting early in the morning, the bar filled with people who were determined to glimpse the invention that everyone talked about enthusiastically but very few had actually seen. I barely ate that day. I was so excited I didn't even go to the movies, which I did every Sunday afternoon, even though the television wouldn't start until seven and the movie finished an hour before. At five I was already in Martiniano's bar (as an exception, he let everyone come in that day, even the kids), sitting in the front row, waiting impatiently for the moment the television would start working.

An hour before the inauguration, you couldn't have

squeezed a toothpick into the bar. Martiniano had piled all
the tables in one corner and used the bar's chairs and some
that a few villagers had brought from home to turn the place
into a makeshift cinema where more than two hundred of
us sat two by two, clustered together like cherries all over the
place. There were people on the floor, on top of the tables,
on the windowsills, and behind the counter. Meanwhile
those who'd had to stay outside (almost twice as many as had
managed to get in) crowded up against each other and
argued with those inside, especially those on top of the
tables, asking them to crouch down so they could see. There
was such a melée that when the time came, Martiniano had
to jump over people to get to the television set to turn it on.

It was at that moment the photographer immortalized us.
I guess it was then, because in the photo Martiniano is standing on a chair and the rest of us are watching him so closely
that we don't even notice—except for one boy, to my right,
who's looking straight at him—the photographer in a corner
taking a picture of us just as Martiniano turns on the television. And so, as I waited to see the faces of the men whose
voices I heard each night on the radio at home, I didn't realize ours were the ones being recorded forever in this photograph which, like Martiniano's television, was in black and
white, even though, many afternoons in the cinema, I saw the
world was already spinning in color. What the photo didn't
capture, but my memory did and so did those of everyone
waiting, like me, to see the television, is that after our long,
patient wait, and despite Martiniano's desperate attempts to
make it work, the only thing we could see on the screen was
a kind of sleet just like that falling on the other side of the
window where the people who couldn't fit in the bar huddled

undaunted. It seems that Martiniano had forgotten to put up the antenna, but we didn't find that out until the next day when a technician came from León to check.

Several years later, in 1969, we relived that scene, although this time in my house and without the Olleros photographer as witness (the arrival of a new television in the village had for some time been as unremarkable as that of a child). Despite that, the day my father bought one— after so much dillydallying that my brothers and sisters and I feared he'd never make up his mind—all the neighbors were in our house for its debut. They weren't really there to watch television, which by now many people had, but to watch the Americans, who were going to land on the moon that night. The landing was scheduled for two o'clock that morning but from eleven our kitchen began filling with people who wanted to see it firsthand. Everyone except Celerina. The old woman went to bed after watching the news, laughing at us for believing in what according to her was a movie—a movie, I remember she said, the Americans were putting on to make us believe they were smarter than the Russians. I didn't manage to find out. I fell asleep waiting and, when I woke up, the transmission was over and most of our guests had left. The television was still on, and the people still there were staring at it as if they could still see the moon on the screen. The only thing I saw before waking up entirely was Celerina's face laughing at us as the sleet on the screen gradually covered her and the world turned into a photograph: the same photo I'm looking at now where Martiniano is still trying to reach the moon.

Translated by Anne McLean

The Invisible Man

Antón Castro

KEN LOACH FILMED *Land and Freedom* in Mirambel. He'd admired the scenery ever since first setting eyes on the Nuns' Gate, the oleander-lined avenue, the narrow streets with their mansions, that early evening atmosphere of yearning and seclusion, where houses float and a diaphanous light made of wind and stillness dissolves. Ken Loach did his utmost to find suitable surroundings: he brought militiamen from all over the country and soldiers from the fascist army who had run through the mountains in pursuit of an enemy target. He is a meticulous man,

ANTÓN CASTRO *(Artexio, A Coruña, 1959–) is a journalist and novelist who has for some time worked in Zaragoza, Aragón, where he edits the weekly cultural supplement of* El Heraldo de Aragón. *He published a prose work in Galician in 1997*—Vida e Morte das Baleias. *His most recent collection of stories in Spanish,* Los seres imposibles *(1998), is in the tradition of the Romantic poet Gustavo Bécquer. Castro organizes annual international literary encounters in the old Arab town of Albarracín. The story here is from* El testamento de amor de Patricio Julve *(1995), in which the writer loosely weaves stories based on events and characters from Aragón around the elusive figure of photographer Patricio Julve.*

cool, focused and firm in his decisions. It's interesting to watch his changing moods: the British gentleman, rather hermetic and solitary, he turns passionate and intense when filming or when he discovers a man of the left, or when he discerns the trace of a heroic deed in a face weather-beaten by pain and danger. Ken Loach knows which side he's on. He knows, and does not doubt, where his historic allegiance lies.

There was a moment when he seemed a little less interested in the filming, as if he'd been struck by a fit of indecision or was overly affected by the daily rivalries between the actors. He and the rest of the crew stayed in the Mirambel guest house, though they held their parties at the Hotel Cantavieja, the same establishment that had once played host to that local character Colonel Balfagón: his soirées, his gallant lovesick odysseys, and his sailor's dream, roving and run aground in the nostalgia of his unfathomable old age. That day, Loach left the set a bit early and headed off to Cantavieja, the city under siege. He sat on the terrace and looked at the rugged natural landscape: the edge of Rebollar, the sharp-peaked mountains, the immaculate white of the rock, the gradual transformation of the hills that disappear off into an indeterminate point like the sea. Ken Loach went inside for a moment and a series of photographs of the town caught his eye. Black-and-white photos of parties, fire bulls, a bailiff with a bronze trumpet pressed to his lips. At first he was fascinated by the sequences, the harsh contrasts, the confidence of the people portrayed before the implacable gaze of the camera. He came back out into the fresh air with a soft drink in hand. Ken Loach returned to the terrace with its panoramic views and kept thinking about the photographs: the unusual serenity of the men (maybe, he thought, they'd been caught unawares), the bold, meticulous framing, the precision of shots that had searched out the ineffable moment. The arrival of his crew interrupted these meditations. Those involved in the film were late because they'd been getting presents ready for him; it was his birthday. The actresses gave him six pairs of faded, torn jeans in different sizes; the actors, some whiskey and two Spanish engagement books. The extras brought him locally made presents: ceramics, tapestries, and miracle-working virgins that made him split his sides with laughter. The most moving gift though was from a farmworker: he presented him with his father's combat uniform, worn in battle under the commands of General Rojo and Enrique Líster, a uniform more than half a century old that smelled not of gunpowder or sweat but of mothballs.

Ken Loach couldn't get the series of photographs out of his head. Fate gave him the perfect alibi. The filming was interrupted for a few days and he announced, against all expectations, that he wouldn't be returning to London or Barcelona like the rest, but would be staying in Cantavieja, at the hotel. He didn't wish to give any explanations. He was curt, distant and stubborn. No one would have understood.

He went back to look at the photos and wrote down a few notes in his Spanish engagement book. It was Mariano, the young proprietor of the hotel, who cleared up one of his doubts.

"I see you like the photos. I should give them to you."

Ken Loach, who was already more than acquainted with the hotelier's generosity, smiled.

"They were taken by Patricio Julve."

"Is he still alive?"

"It's hard to say. But it's been a long time since he's been around here. If he's not dead, he must be very old."

Far from satisfying him, that tiny revelation only increased Loach's curiosity. He went back up to his room more intrigued than ever. He seemed possessed by the spirit of the photographs.

The next morning his only words were: "Mariano, who could tell me about Patricio Julve?"

He began an exhaustive session of visits and inquiries. He spoke not only with the old folks but also with all those who had requested Patricio Julve's services. He went down to the farms, he visited the cemetery several times, the Agrarian Cooperative and its archives, where they have comprehensive collections on rural life in the area (scythers, road workers, shepherds, farmworkers, etc.); he visited Barranco de San Juan, the estates of Umbría Negra, the Mas de Palomo and its indescribable inhabitant, María Tena, who sometimes seemed to remember even things she hadn't lived through. He made fast friends with the gravedigger Basilio Monforte, who showed him his wedding photos, subtly retouched. He went to all the rectories, found the clandestine photos of the murder of the priest Urbano Oliver and even resorted to going through several newspaper archives. In a mere week, Ken Loach seemed a changed man. He returned to the hotel with folders, framed photographs, group shots, impressive individual portraits, and then he stayed up until the small hours making notes and comparing shots.

It was inconceivable that an Englishman, who spoke only broken Spanish, had managed to get hold of (even for a few days) such a complete collection of photographs.

One night after dinner, Mariano and Ken Loach were left alone. The hotelier sat down at his table and said: "If I'm going to give you those photos, at least give me the consolation of knowing something about the man who took them."

Ken Loach hesitated, but after an instant said: "I don't know if I dare, Mariano. First of all, I have to ask you to forgive any inaccuracies and geographical imprecision. You have to realize what I'm going to tell you is like a myth, almost a dream. Barely anything is known for certain about Patricio Julve. If it weren't for the piles of photographs he's left around the world, we'd know nothing. I want you to know all I've managed is to tie a few loose threads together, link up testimonies. It seems clear that he was born in a small village in the Ebro basin, in the province of Zaragoza. It didn't take long to see he was no ordinary child; he was shy and quite housebound. His mother would say to him, before she went out to the fields in her wagon: "Patricio, you can't come out to the plot with me today, it's too cold. Wait for me here and don't go too close to the fire." She'd come home and find him there still in the same spot, happy and flushed, like an angel. But he was soon struck by misfortune. A long and unpleasant illness left him with only one good leg. In Spanish I think you call it a *tumor blanco;* Patricio Julve was certainly lame. And you perhaps knew that already, Mariano. But his calamities didn't end there: it was a long time before it became known, but as a child he lost the sight in his left eye.

"Why did he take up photography? It's a difficult question to answer. He went to study in Zaragoza (and not in Teruel, as a few of my informants have insisted), thanks to the fact that a middle-class, childless man gave him a room in his house. This man, known simply as Moneva, took a shine to the boy: he saw he was intelligent, studious, and mechanically inclined. The period was one of great progress for photography (and bear in mind, I'm talking about 1910 or the early twenties), especially for several studios that flourished in the city, specializing in retouching and manipulating negatives. There were whole families dedicated to this. Women were especially adept. It was an enterprise as arduous as it was beautiful: they could, for example, dress a beggar in a velveteen suit, they could invent an imaginary island inside a family's kitchen or add exotic landscapes by technical processes. Patricio Julve was an expert in the tricks of the laboratory, a master of special effects, although he never lost any sleep over such things. What he liked were straightforward photos, the unerring shot of a face or a group of people.

"His career seemed headed toward the art of retouching, as I said, or studio photography. I should add another detail about Patricio Julve's personality: he was a restless and kindhearted man who was fond of adventure. For him life was a volcano in permanent eruption, and he came to the conclusion that all the beauty in the world could be captured by an eye—one eye alone. These kinds of phrases tend to be repeated. I'm telling you all this so you understand why a handicapped, completely unknown man went off to Paris to study photography and complete his apprenticeship in the production of postcards. I don't know exactly how long he spent there. Perhaps three or four years, and it fills me with pride to tell you that he also traveled to my country. He spent two months in London. I've got a revelation for you, Mariano: Patricio Julve left not a single known snapshot of either Paris or London. I've been wondering these days if perhaps he hadn't liked big cities. It could be. After a few years, of which we know very little, except that he frequented many museums and markets, he returned to Zaragoza. The most surprising thing about him on his return was not his knowledge of photography, not by a long shot, but something unexpected: a bicycle with a fixed sprocket. Well, a bicycle and a Globus wooden box camera. I'm not sure of the dimensions but it might well have been 13 by 18 or even bigger, particularly if we take into account that Patricio Julve produced his early work accompanied by a mule-drawn wagon and a saffron-colored spaniel. And it seems he produced them in this exact place, from the vulture perches and snowcapped mountains of Cuarto Pelado.

"Patricio Julve's life is a mystery. Some reports I've been given suggest that he worked for local newspapers and magazines. I haven't been able to confirm that. I've also been told that he was magnificent at recording architectural works. I don't know but it's not difficult to surmise. His shots of the Matutano palace in Iglesuela del Cid are enough to prove it: he captures the details of the imperial stairway beneath a sinuous play of light and shadow, the bed with its lordly canopy, the decrepit mirrors of the washstand reflecting the coffered ceiling, the lamps and those landscape frescoes with their agricultural and taurine motifs. Suddenly, for no apparent reason, the spell was cast.

Or, I should say, the love affair with these lands. Patricio Julve was the great artist of these realms. First he put his bicycle on the roofrack of the *Cayman*, the postal truck, and went everywhere. He took snapshots of Ejulve, Villarluengo, Mirambel, Cantavieja, and Iglesuela del Cid, as I said. When the car couldn't reach a headland in the mountains or a village perched up in the rocks, Patricio Julve pedaled up. No obstacles stood in his way: the old folks remember him climbing flights of steps, outcrops, crags. And a member of the Gascón family from Mas de Diego, with a head like a calendar because he remembers not just events but dates and times of day, told me that he remembered him, just before the war, climbing up on top of the farmhouse roof to get some aerial shots one day during the harvest, with his damaged leg and crutch. The threshing floors along the valley unfolded into a gentle gully on the other side of the house, and it had turned into a tumult of people, machines, and animals. In three pictures Patricio Julve captured the dirty sheep, the horses, and dogs among the straw hats of the peasants, and an asphyxiating dust that rose from the earth.

"I think he was a very ingenious artist. He liked to experiment with light and materials, what we now call media: different types of paper, tinting, pushing the film, and other fiddly little things. He particularly liked to take children's photos at dawn or dusk. He'd ask the family to set two or three very bright bonfires and he'd arrange the kids on chairs or in front of a suitable backdrop, whether a cart or some more or less evocative woodsheds. And that's how he'd photograph them, with that indescribable veneer, half bronze, half firelight. That's why his portraits are so disquieting and yet so beautiful; they have an aura and magic. I wouldn't know how to answer some questions: it's not known for certain where he lived. There are those who claim to have seen him in a small studio in Zaragoza, a studio with views of San Juan de los Panetes and the towers of the Pilar cathedral. There are those who claim he shared a tiny place with another photographer who hasn't gone down in history as an artist but as a casualty of a wartime firing squad, a certain Martín Mormeneo. I don't even know, and believe me I am truly sorry I don't, how people got in touch with him. It's as if he possessed a sixth sense or had the gift of clairvoyance. Basilio Monforte thinks he remembers him appearing all of a sudden once they'd decided to hang daguerreotypes on the crosses in the cemetery in Cantavieja.

"I've searched for other pieces of his work far from this region. I've asked if anyone remembers a portrait photographer with a limp who went about on a bicycle. Nobody could give me any information except for a guy named Coyne who told me that years ago there'd been a magnificent Aragonese documentary photographer, Juan Mora I think he said he was called, who also had a limp and a special bicycle. What a coincidence! Sometimes I've wondered, Mariano, if they weren't the same person; I've thought that Patricio Julve never existed or that he was an invisible man. Why this urge to hide? After his last session, an admirable series of portraits he took of a young woman called Raquel, he vanished again leaving no trace but that inventory of irresistible beauty. I think after that he disappeared for good. Looking at those photos I wanted to imagine he'd died of love or despair in a ravine one early morning. Of love because he could never hope to see up close a creature as beautiful again and of despair because those pictures are the trace of a glorious and unrepeatable instant, that fleeting moment in which the cold lens takes on the soul or consciousness of a lover. Those photos are an elegy or a testament of love.

"I've told you, Mariano, that I came to believe that Patricio Julve was an invisible man. I thought he was a chimera, a phantom fed by the solitude of these sierras, a collective dream superimposed with different photographs. But in the end, loathing the enigma and resigned to this cowardly consideration, I found an incredible document in Mas de Palomo. A document that is both a testimony and irrefutable proof: perhaps the only self-portrait of a genius. This. Look."

Ken Loach handed over a picture. The hotelier looked at the photo. It was a postcard shrouded in ochre tones. He saw a chubby boy barely two years old, Colonel Balfagón, and a lame man, balancing a box camera on a crutch. Mariano recognized himself and Patricio Julve. He turned the paper over and read aloud: "Cantavieja. Day of Our Lady, 1967."

The night had grown calm, dark, and bereft of stars.

Translated by Anne McLean

The Dog
Miguel Delibes

THE SUN SHONE DOWN too luminously for an October morning, and the short, miserable man sought relief in the dwarf oak's scant shade. Two steps on, a lean man, neck puckered by an enormous scar, drank eagerly from a wineskin the other man had just handed him. After he'd finished, he wiped his lips with the back of his right hand, squinted and stared into the distance. The hillside dropped off steeply toward the river, which glittered between two lines of moribund poplars. Old, rusty Laffosete shotguns lay on the ground next to their cartridge belts, a limp partridge hanging from one. The dog was panting at their side, a dark-brown, taciturn-eyed animal giving an untimely display of her grossly dis-

---

MIGUEL DELIBES *(1920–) is among the most outstanding literary figures of contemporary Spanish literature. His first novel,* La sombra del ciprés es alargada *(1947), won the Nadal Prize. He creates an original Spanish, preserving rural or colloquial language in his portrayal of poor peasants and marginalized youth from northern Castile, in such novels as* Las ratas *(1962) and* El camino *(1950). This story is from the collection of stories,* La Mortaja *(1970), written between 1948 and 1963.*

tended udders. The scarred man, his back at odds with the rugged hillside, turned calmly round and looked the animal over.

"She's getting on," he said. "What did you do with her puppies?" The dog anxiously sniffed at the partridge and two weightless feathers floated off on the wind. The mouth of the left barrel of one gun was dented. The short, miserable man's trousers had patched knees and ragged bottoms. The short, miserable man reached out a scrawny, misshapen hand to stroke the animal repeatedly between the ears. The dog stopped panting, shut her mouth, and looked intelligently at her master.

"She's not old," he replied: "Giving birth wears her out. This time she had seven and I only let her keep two. Loy isn't old. I threw the other five into the river."

"Weren't they pedigree?" inquired the scarred man, sitting down wearily in the luminous morning sun.

"Well," said the other man, "I wanted her to mate with Leo's pointer but she always goes to that lousy shepherd dog, Tiger. I don't like doing it, but I had to drown five puppies in the river."

"She's getting long in the tooth," the scarred man insisted, as the hillside pained his back. "She's lost her nose."

The short, miserable man lifted his damp gaze from the animal's eyes and directed it defiantly into the other man's eyes.

"You've seen her in the field, you shouldn't say that. There's not a dog in the village like Loy. Loy is intelligent and hardworking. You've seen her and you shouldn't say such things."

The short, miserable man pointed at the skinny partridge. The only sound was the breeze rustling through the oak's slender branches.

"It's her job. I didn't get a shot all morning. That's her job."

The short, miserable man tried irony. He said: "Loy can't show partridges where there are none. She's either too old or too young for that."

To no avail the scarred man tried to get his head in the shade of the oak. He added: "I can never forget Demetrio's bitch. When I talk about hunting dogs, Demetrio's dog always comes to mind. If I owned a dog that ran off, I'd string it up. I wouldn't put up with it."

The short, miserable man who was drinking from the wineskin choked. A reddish line trickled down his chin and fell on to his shirtfront. He ignored it.

"My bitch doesn't run off," he retorted angrily. "Do you know what Don Feliciano says whenever he goes hunting with her? He says: 'You should be proud: she does everything but talk.' That's Don Feliciano and I don't reckon he's a nobody."

The bitch watched her master indulgently. Down below, on the other side of the river, a church belfry emerged from the willows. A gust of hot wind hit the chaparral. The man with the scarred neck locked his fingers together patiently.

"Demetrio's bitch always hunted alongside you," he said. "If her ears twitched and her tail waved you could ignore her, but if it went as stiff as a brush, you could be sure there was game. And she never got impatient, no siree. She waited as long as necessary. She was one-eyed, but her good eye never wandered from the game or the hunter. You had to say *'Vamos'* to get her to move. She always hunted next to you."

The short, misshapen man appeared self-absorbed. He

couldn't hear the husky whisper of the other's voice. He thought: *I couldn't live without this animal.* They shared the same room, the same lack of company; he had gotten used to the animal's habits and favorite haunts. He even forgave her for giving him litters by Tiger rather than by Leo's pointer. Every night he fell asleep on his bunk contemplating the patient mass of the animal curled up on the floor. He told himself: *She fetches partridges in a flash, with just one look from me. Last year she got me that duck out of the river in December. She's never angry if I miss. It was a poor year for partridges and Loy can't get around that. She tries even though she knows it's useless. And come to think of it, doesn't Demetrio's bitch stretch out when she sees nothing's doing?*

The scarred man got up wearily, calmly picked his gunbelt up from the ground and strapped it round his waist. The cartridge heads stuck out, strangely wrapped in cigarette papers. He said with resignation: "There was a time when you could live from hunting. Today we can't and the hunt can't. Hares lie low like dormice and without a bloodhound there's no way you can flush them out."

The village clustered round the church tower beneath them. The poplars still carried fading yellow leaves. Nonetheless the sun was too luminous for an October day. The short, miserable man stood up and the bitch followed suit licking his heels. The short, miserable man was beginning to hate the man with the white scar. As he picked up his gun with the dented barrel, he said: "There's a shortage of partridges. My dog's not short on scent."

The lean man replied as he eyed the inhospitable expanse of hillside: "If the partridges smelled like your feet, I wouldn't need a dog to hunt them out."

They walked silently, patiently, a thirty-yard gap between

them. The short, miserable man followed the high ridge of the hillside. He walked whistling quietly from time to time. When she heard him, the dog turned her head to look at him. He returned the look and the two pairs of eyes reflected a pious mutual understanding. *She's lost her nose, she's lost her nose. How's she going to hunt partridges where there are none?* he said to himself and contemplated the thin silhouette, wineskin dangling from the man's waist, progressing painfully across the steep incline. The short man walked slowly, stamped on the heather, stuck the barrels of his gun among the scrub, left no shrub untouched. Now and then he whistled softly. The dog's distended udders created a painful impression of exhaustion. Her wearisome panting alone disturbed the peaceful morning. Down below, pitched close to the ground, the village's modest adobe houses clung to the church tower. The river glittered between the poplars.

The hare rushed out from underneath the short, miserable man's feet without the dog even noticing. As the short, miserable man took aim he hoped the scarred man hadn't noticed Loy's slip. The hare was done for and the short, miserable man had it in his treacherous sights. It was then that the dog intervened.

The short, miserable man's open eye spotted Loy's skull in the same line of fire as the hare. He thought about not shooting but the scarred man was yelling and waving from halfway down the hill. He swore quietly. The short, miserable man knew the dog was making a dreadful mistake. And when he shot, he did so knowing the dog and hare were one and the same target. The report echoed off the hillside to the village, and while it resounded, the short, miserable man heard the dog howl a few steps away. He wasn't surprised to see the animal stretched out, head bloody, back legs convulsing. The hare lay still, next to a clump of heather, four yards away. The short man came over and wistfully stroked his dog's back with a skinny, misshapen hand. He was startled by the scarred man's voice at his side.

"She was past it; it's just as well," he said.

The short, miserable man thought of the two puppies waiting for him by the hearth. Then, when the dog stopped moving, he slowly looked up, sought out his companion's eyes, went on stroking, and said: "Did you see how she pointed?"

The scarred man, his face turned toward the overly luminous sky, drank from the wineskin. When he'd finished, he wiped his lips with the back of his hand, picked the hare up and squeezed its back until it urinated. Then he continued calmly, aware he felt sorry for the short, miserable man: "I was on another track; I didn't see a thing. I was on another track."

The short, miserable man closed his eyes, dazzled by the glittering river or perhaps deadened by the presence of the dead dog. Unaware he was lying, he said: "The animal waited until I'd caught up with her. She pointed so stiffly I could have sat on her. Do you hear me? I didn't because I didn't feel like it. '*Vamos*,' I told her. I remembered what you'd said about Demetrio's dog."

"Come on," the other said casually. "We can still make a morning of it."

The sun stirred too brightly high above them and the river sparkled in the steep valley between the two lines of stiff poplars.

Translated by Peter Bush

What Happened in Atajo

José Jiménez Lozano

THIS IS WHAT HAPPENED IN ATAJO: after a time, a man drove up in a car; and, when he drove up, an official in the small town hall office was waiting for him, as if he had an appointment with him, and he showed him all around the town, and he twirled his helmet a lot. Then the man left, and the small-town official said to the small-town mayor, Señor Isidro: "Atajo just hit the jackpot. They're going to build a tourist complex here, made to look like an old inn, but with every modern convenience; money is going flow into this town like water."

The mayor, however, said he wasn't signing anything until he'd talked to the townspeople, and until everything was crystal clear.

JOSÉ JIMÉNEZ LOZANO *(1930–) was born in Langa, Avila, Spain in 1930. He is the author of nine novels and numerous critical essays and short stories. He has published three collections of poetry:* Tantas devastaciones *(Valladolid, 1992),* Un fulgor tan breve *(Madrid, 1995), and* El tiempo de Eurídice *(Valladolid, 1996) and has received several important literary awards. This text is an excerpt from the novel* Un hombre en la raya, *which parodies the capriciousness of tourist development in an imaginary Castilian village.*

"But it's already crystal clear!" the official said.

First, they would repair the access roads. They would re-route the shortcut into town, to make it accessible by car. Then they'd start work on the town itself: the church, the streets, the houses.

"They won't flood everything and build a reservoir?" the mayor asked.

"No. What would be the point of fixing everything up if they were going to do that?"

"Who knows. They like flooding towns, right?"

But no, there was to be no reservoir. What there was going to be was a hotel, plain and simple.

"And where are they going to build it?"

But that was another issue altogether, the official said. The architect who had come hadn't decided yet, or if he had, he hadn't told the official. But it didn't matter where it was. It would bring up the price of land, guarantee work for the townspeople, and they wouldn't have to worry about their children's futures anymore. That much was clear. And Señor Isidro, the mayor, made him repeat all this several times so he could explain it to everyone when they had their meeting, but then he thought better of it and told the official that it would be preferable if he, or the man who had driven up in the car, explained it all to them.

The national media—press, radio, and television—reported the planning of a hotel in Atajo that would be some sort of Theban desert refuge where bankrupt businessmen, politicians, writers, and artists could find the peace and quiet they so desperately needed. But getting to Atajo was not straightforward, and access had to be straight; water and electricity supplies were very poor, and lines had to be re-laid; it was a tepid town, featureless and lacking in character, and required remodeling from top to bottom; not just the buildings, but the streets, too. The church had to be restored, and even the sad old shepherd's cabin was to be converted into an exotic hangout, some sort of pagoda with a sand garden that could double as a chic tea room.

The projected hotel was to have just twenty rooms, and of those six would be special suites for special guests, who would also have their own separate dining room; in general, however, everything was planned so that all of the guests could enjoy their solitude if they wanted solitude, yet find companionship with no trouble if that was what struck their fancy. They discussed having areas to accommodate groups, for meetings and conferences and the like, but that idea was jettisoned. This would be a place for solitude, solitude in which you could see a movie if you felt like it, or play sports. The "committee of specialists"—made up of mostly architects, but also of psychologists and of experts in art, interior design, cuisine, hygiene, nutrition, sound, and other areas—theorized that what was needed was a complex sensitive "to modern man's most profound needs": the need for physical and mental rest and relaxation, contact with nature, and "group solitude," which of course should be balanced and peaceful. And to achieve all of that, absolutely everything had to be carefully considered: the color of the walls and wall-to-wall carpeting in the rooms, the design and color of every stick of furniture, lighting, as well as plain physical comfort, the elegance of apparently—but only apparently—insignificant objects such as light switches and doorhandles.

Needless to say, the building would be part glass and aluminum, part brick and stone; the sound proofing would be flawless, yet simultaneously equipped to pick up on all the sounds of nature. Some argued for certain species of exotic birds that would adapt easily to the environment, others insisted that nothing whatsoever should disturb the ambience. There were those who proposed antique sculptures or paintings as a decorative touch, but most thought that true mental relaxation could only be attained via abstract painting and a purely sculptural display of shapes for the simple reason that conventional and classic art always stimulated feelings and reactions, while nonfigurative art was the simple contemplation of meaningless forms, with the undeniable ability to evoke serenity.

Clearly the issue of the local residents was also broached, because although obviously the visitors would not live with the townsfolk, and in fact would happen upon them only by chance, they really must not give off an air of ragtag poverty, or even slovenliness or neglect; the same went for their homes, which the residents might—one never knew—be curious to have a peek at. Quite the contrary, the local inhabitants had to appear stylish and urbane, and that was problematic. First, they had to determine how many inhabitants there should be, and determine their lifestyles. Second, they needed to somehow recycle people; so, in general, people of a certain age, who by virtue of their age were no longer recyclable, had to be put in old people's homes, or transferred to other villages; villages that were rather far away because those that were close to Atajo, inside the perimeter of the great valley formed by the surrounding peaks, would go the way of Atajo. And of course they had to think about future generations, which meant that at the school in the neighboring town all of the local children's education would have the same orientation: the privileged destiny of inhabitants of Atajo, an important and integral part of the burgeoning human and geographical landscape.

The church was another matter altogether. No doubt, total restoration was in order. Research studies, samples, and soundings so far had showed it was an early Romanesque gem, and they'd found gothic paintings at the entrance to the tower stairs, and on one of the walls of what had once been the baptistery—in the stairway, a skeleton carrying a coffin, and in the baptistery, the Pietà, or Descent from the Cross. Numerous decisions would have to be made. The first was the restoration of the church, though not with the aim of continuing worship, but rather with the aim of preserving the artistic gem that it was, minus the worship; then they would build a little chapel in the outskirts of town for the dozen or so old folks who still went to church. This was particularly important because, if they didn't build the little chapel, the bishopric most likely would not hand over the church; if they did build it, however, the concession would not be a problem, and would cost next to nothing, since concrete churches—ones that looked like silos, parking complexes, and industrial units—were all the rage. It was crucial that it have neon lights and a stained glass window that looked like a jigsaw puzzle and two or three cast-iron Christs or Virgins. That had already been discussed and was pretty much agreed upon, as was the giving over of the church bells and the hand bells—not only from Atajo but also from nearby villages—which would theoretically be hung from a huge stone steeple construction at the entrance to the town, as a unique monument to ancient culture, and an electric-powered carillon that would ring on certain, very special occasions, once the anthropologists and folklore specialists had determined the significance of chiming bells in days of yore, and the contemporary meaning it could and should now have.

With respect to the paintings, the majority of the committee felt inclined to move them to a museum, for a number of reasons, ranging from the fact that keeping gothic paintings in a renovated Romanesque church didn't make much sense, to the consideration that paintings of a rather fundamentalist religious nature were seen to be out of sync with the peace-and-tranquility atmosphere they wanted to imbue everything with, and that the paintings handled their subjects cadaverously, crudely, and a touch morbidly. CRAS ET TU MORIES, read the tower stairway painting, and MORTUUS EST PRO NOBIS read the other, and anyone could translate those inscriptions. It wasn't at all pleasant—nor was it psychologically healthy—to fixate on so much death and guilt. "What was Man guilty of? What?" asked the committee members. Then there was the fact that the fine arts bigwigs seemed fascinated by the frescoes, and the Church was only too happy to hand them over to a museum because in their estimation they no longer served any pastoral purpose; all the Church insisted on keeping was the baroque imagery, which was felt to be valuable for popular religiosity. But they showed an absolute disinterest in holding onto the altarpiece depicting Christ's Descent with its life-sized, clothed, moveable statues, which had served at Good Friday services for centuries; the committee thought it could be moved to whatever chapel was built, so as not to break with a tradition that, once fittingly adapted, might become an interesting spectacle that would doubtless bring the people of Atajo together, at least as long as the old folks were still around. They'd put on a religious play, an *auto*, with professional actors and theater technicians, even perform it in the church itself, which would be a fantastic setting, with a script written by a significant, modish author so that the whole thing struck a chord with current sensibilities, bearing in mind that, if well done, the play could attract not just the public at large, but also the select guests that "the solitude-seekers" this their Thebes might invite, or even famous foreigners passing through Spain.

The final item to consider was the little cemetery, behind the church and right in the middle of town. They clearly had to close it and wrench out all those iron crosses so it could be turned into a grassy area, but this was not as easy as one might think, given the scant cultural savvy of these folk; their antiquated ideas about death meant that they would not stand by and allow (as sometimes happens to human remains found in old churches and monasteries) all the bones be buried together in one deep hole, let alone be burned, an even more hygienic solution. But if there was no alternative and they had to shift the dead to the new cemetery—and there could be no alternative if they didn't want to fluster the town and even neighboring villages—then that was the first thing they had to take care of. And if the people accepted the grave transfer plan, then 90 percent of the Atajo transformation battle was won. Then they could tackle the second step, the celebration of Christ's Descent without any traditional imagery and with professional actors, who were already being selected; and if that went through as well, the rest would be a piece of cake. Nobody, but nobody, should find out anything, and nobody did, because after the visit from the man who drove up in the car and spoke to the official in the small town hall office, no other outsiders had been seen, and neither the priest nor the official had received any news, and the rumors and gossiping about Atajo's transformation stopped, and the media—press, radio, and television—reports went silent, too. Neighboring villages said, "Seems like Atajo's not selling its Christ after all. No gravy train for you."

Translated by Lisa Dillman

Mamá
Javier Puebla

NIGHT FALLS. Night. And all the telephone booths in Plaza de Lavapiés fill up.

The old bolero singer who now sells cocaine in the bars.

The Moroccan Mafioso who married a Spanish woman and was transmuted by love into a security guard.

The Korean woman who sold you a beer in the deli a short time ago.

The forty-something punk who keeps dreaming himself Peter Pan.

The cop who's been patrolling the plaza all afternoon to prevent disturbances.

JAVIER PUEBLA *(1958–) was born in Madrid, where he now lives after many years in New York, Barcelona, Dakar, and Murcia. The first writer ever to undertake the ambitious project of writing a story each day for an entire year ("Mamá" is number 125), he has worked as a journalist and diplomat, and has also written two novels and two books of short stories. Lavapiés, the neighborhood portrayed in "Mamá," has seen many changes; once considered the city's most "authentically" madrileño barrio, it is now home to large immigrant communities and has become the most multicultural area in Madrid.*

The student of fine arts who is terrified at the thought of having to return to Germany.

The scriptwriter who just drank a beer in *Pakesteis* after wasting a fortune at a peep show on Calle Atocha.

The woman who from her balcony spies on couples making love and imagines that she is the girl involved.

Each one on the phone, in a booth, in Plaza de Lavapiés. When night falls. Night. And if one could silence the noise of the motors, the murmur of the televisions, and the pleas of those who pray, one could hear, coming out of the mouths glued to the mouthpieces, and in many different languages—Russian, Spanish, Chinese, Arabic, German, Senegalese—one word repeated more often than any other. Mamá.

Translated by Cola Franzen

Siesta Light

Rosa Chacel

THE LIGHT COMING IN now through the dormer is siesta-time light, and the silence is like a tribute to its dominion, which spreads throughout the whole neighborhood. The light coming in now through the dormer has a benevolent but imperious look. Who could resist it? This light looks at the neighborhood in a hypnotizing fashion, imposing a truce on the effort, on the labor implied in looking. Its fullness and its force can be managed only by muting it, by filtering it through various screens in various places. Green blinds, sensitive to the wind, trembling like poplar trees. White curtains, as nuptial as mosquito nets; opalescent muslins. Transparent window shades of waxed

ROSA CHACEL *(Valladolid, 1898–Madrid, 1994) went into exile in 1938 during the civil war and lived in Rio de Janeiro and Buenos Aires, where she collaborated with* Sur *and translated Racine and Mallarmé. She returned to Spain in 1971 and was awarded the Critics Prize in 1976. Her novels* The Memoirs of Leticia Valle *(1945) and* The Maravillas District *(1976) offer new approaches to the writing of fiction and autobiography. The second novel recreates the daily life of two girls and their families who live in a small apartment in a district of 1920s Madrid, full of light and aromas.*

cloth with brilliant, gloomily brilliant, colors, oval-shaped
wreaths of roses framing autumn forests with running
deer, oaks or fields or lakes with swans. Intense green in
the landscapes, the livid reds of the roses. The light at this
time of day is filtered through those screens and looks
upon tidy rooms, fluffed-up beds, uncovered bodies. Its
look is acquiescent, its countenance harmonious with
each window dressing. The dormer has no dressing; it is
simply bare, unadorned and open. This light is also acquiescent toward what is unadorned, open to mere necessity.
The light doesn't come in to be seen, but to fulfill its mission, and its aspect, its demeanor at siesta time is not all
that different from working hours. Its demeanor is neither
benign nor aggressive. It is attentive, modest, never dazzling, but solicitously enlightening—Isabel would never
have discovered it here, would never have contemplated
its nakedness here. The light arrives with the dawn and
looks pallidly at covered things: the two sleepers, bundled
in their beds, the little household utensils covered with
cloths. Their owner doesn't leave uncovered the things
that don't want to be seen; it is decorous to cover them,
and uncovering them as the growing light permits is like
attending their birthing, their coming to light. The light
gazes on what appears very clean, brilliant, as it is uncovered. The light corroborates it, puts it in its place. The
room has been seen in all its incarnations by the hard,
strict, necessary light of poverty—the light that saw them
arrive with their bundles, with their elementary, insuffi-
cient possessions, which have gradually been transformed,
growing and improving thanks to skillful combinations—
the skills and crafts of the spider, the thriftiness of the ant,

the cleverness of the weasel—all products of sacred maternal zeal; an art, or rather, a handicraft: creation. Nature—woman—abhors a vacuum; she feels, she sees—the supreme abstraction—what is lacking, what is needed, and invests herself with the power to create from nothingness, to make whatever is lacking so that lack will not exist because the nonexistence that is lack is mortal. Necessity dictates the work, works the soil for her after fruitless searches, degrading and debilitating, but not sufficiently so to exhaust her zeal. The saddest, most desolate light has smiled an instant, has winked to signal possibilities in the negotiations with an even greater poverty, with a senility that ceded territory, gave half its space in exchange for a bit of assistance. The light, after that transaction, was also linked here with a smell—odor, a fleeting material that escapes without breaking bonds, without erasing itself on the way, but on the contrary, being the path to the fragrant object—the smell of need, of sustenance. . . . Once the room was ceded and the door between the two rooms blocked, the morning light—hard, strict, corroborative, and collaborative—joined in essential accommodation with the steam of the little kettle on the oil stove, with the oil itself, with the chemical substances that serve hygiene—bleach, disinfectant, yellow soap saturating the hemp scouring pad. . . . Odors as cruel as guardians, as stern as protective watchmen, are sometimes conquered by sensual, seductive cooking smells: garlic and onion, bay leaf, pepper. . . . Confused with these aromas, the light abdicates its silence—the silence of a district with little traffic; only hawkers' cries rise from the deep street—and welcomes the busy noise of a Singer sewing machine. This necessary harmony stays inside the room. Outside, in the long attic hallway, the light is more leisurely, its mission is not so pressing because no one there needs lighting. Here the light grows sparer—not from parsimony, a concept antithetical to light—because it localizes or systematizes its beams Rembrandt-style; it falls from little round openings through which soft, heavy, silent cats drop in. The cats fall from them like drops of rain, falling by their own weight and hitting the floor with an imperceptible thud, then running down the hall. There they look for their prey or their adventures and leap with precision through the little window that gives access to the roof. The light there, in the long corridor lined by the garret doors, running the length of the house—the corner between the Calles San Vicente and San Andrés: five garrets facing toward San Vicente and five toward San Andrés—in the long hall, the light assumes the violent chiaroscuro and the dark, ferocious, sharp smell of the cats. Inside the garrets the light scarcely touches old trunks, broken baskets, tin basins, portraits of people long dead and bronze objects long out of fashion. Then on the staircase there's the scattering of the vertical illumination of the skylight. It's magnanimous at any hour. Resplendent at midday, it is almost overwhelming on the top floor: merciless at the end of the climb. And every floor—each floor has two apartments—has its own kind of light or at least has its own conversation with light, because the light in each quiet corner takes on the demeanor that the dialogue elicits: in each space it takes on the disposition of the whole: the color of the walls, of the furniture and of the faces,

because certain specific pieces of furniture harmonize
with the style of the food. Certain cuisines give blood a
certain color, which affects the face. But not just through
the blood, no: there is a tone inspired by appetite or the
lack of it, by pleasure or accomodation, by resignation or
habit, which is the enemy of the senses. All these tones
mark human flesh the way curtains color light and both of
them—cuisines with their heavy or stimulating spices,
and curtains hanging dark and heavy over the sashes or
agreeably white with little cupids embroidered on the
edges, give the color of their blood to the light: lively, reddish, or somber, or insipid. But going step by step and
leaving aside all defining adjectives—which are always ex-
tremely ambitious, tireless, and stubborn: let's leave them
aside—the color of the light, the blood of the light on
each floor is—concretely on the floor that now concerns
us—the taciturn, dusty light that slides off bookstands
heavy with knowledge in a small room where an illustrious mathematician has just carried out vital calculations.
A small dwelling, a library, an eating space, a sleeping area
with a large, still-shared marriage bed. Still—after more
than fifty years—harboring what was a lovingly discor-
dant couple. Concretely . . . it's so difficult to say something concretely: concreteness limits, and limiting is
negative, but delimiting is positive. Ah, how can we de-
limit without limiting? Above all, if what is being out-
lined is a very singular and individual uniqueness. At any
rate, concretely, in the small room—third on the right—
two old folks maintain their discord and care for it like an
only daughter, always a little girl as far as the parents are
concerned, preserving the conflictive youth of a studious

man and a frivolous woman, of an austere, sallow, sober, and disciplined body and a rosy restless body that consumes sweets and tangles of yarn in a quick whispering of needles as well as "ladies" news concerning other peoples' lives and loves. The laborious discord is attenuated now by new attachments. The light is lit when it begins to get dark. Electric light—is it a hired light or simply light like all light? It's turned on in the late afternoon and creeps into the hallway, accompanied by a nice smell, although a bit somber and melancholy. It's nice because it's new, melancholy because of the wintry and very strong flavor of celery. It spreads through the hallway, little by little, just a bit ahead of the steam from the two cups in which two cubes of Maggi are dissolving in boiling water. The light is more complex and more hard to define in the room to the left. Very different times are arranged, not according to a hierarchy, but according to effect—and thus they create very different effects of light. There is a feminine time—not maternal but matronly. This accounts for the partial subjugation, or frustration, of the hegemony of present time in favor of the nominal rank of former times. Concretely, to follow the rooms laid out along the third-floor hallway that runs parallel to Calle San Andrés, the final redoubt of the building, fortified by respect for a prestigious past, Aunt's room is first. The title Aunt has supplanted a name, Doña Marina, that merely served as a social denomination of the person who remained infertile in her brilliant life as a governor's wife. The light in her room splashes off small and finely woven baskets, made by Indians on far-off islands, and blends lovingly with the smell of aromatic resins, revealing the exquisite tones of a cashmere shawl and the polished yellows of an ivory Christ. In the rest of the dwelling the light wavers, changing its aspect in the different rooms. It enters the kitchen like a servant or a workman. The open window to the right of the cookstove allows the sun to reflect off the opposite wall and the pots hung by the hearth shine in response. The light and smells play rather than blend. It's an interplay of spices from all Spain's territories, perhaps the only form of nostalgia in the ruler of this domain, for she doesn't make a cult of the past. That is, she maintains a cult, but it's for a past that never passed—that never happened, to be more precise. Seas and lands traveled stayed *there* because she never got *here*, never thought she was living in the present. She lived thinking of a very near future, something that was about to come and never came. Thus, lands overseas lost their category of memories because what was lived in the past never took place. The light, indecisive, creeps through the house of a person who always considered herself a grand dame, a prima donna in the home of a genius, and assumes its own characteristics only in the study with the piano. In the study the light is pleasant and clear. It does its duty shining on worn-out exercises and scores—it carried out its mission for twenty years on scored sheets of paper, shining on the rapid writing and on the even more rapid thought, helping it run with its butterfly net throughout the room. It is only in this room—with its balcony facing San Vicente— that the light has known the present, the real, and has shone upon something that really was. Of course, on that was built the uncertain future; but there were real, although momentary, illuminations. These stayed on and

remain still—in the dreams of Ariadne (the light sometimes shines through her waxy, alabaster blood), in the
pensive artist whom a modest artisan painted in a friendly
oil—his hair not yet gray—before his premature absence.
Frustration, escape, one might say. Or a sentence passed
by adversity. We said twenty years, but it was thirty or
over thirty, perhaps half a century. At that time there was
no oil painting, mediocre but faithful, on the wall above
the piano, because his hair was not yet gray: it was youthful, Espronceda-like. The hands were elongated and very
slim. They toiled every day religiously upon the keyboard.
It couldn't be more exact to say that the young maestro
worked like a slave . . . forced by passion, by the force that
gave him the energy to try to be perfect. There, then, the
light—spring days with the half-closed balcony, maternal
carnations arranged on the railing—paid homage to the
exceptionally perfect notes. On winter afternoons with
the pitter-patter of rain or the silence of the snow the
light was modest and left intact the dark corners that har-
bored the violence of *La Apassionata.*

Translated by d.a. démers

Gran Vía

Rafael Chirbes

LOOKS WERE ALL IMPORTANT. Jacket, tie, cologne, saying the right thing—oh, please, allow me. "A man's image is everything. One man stands out from the next by the impression he makes. Stark naked they're all the same: open them up and inside they're stinking sacks of shit." That's what Captain Varela back in Zaragoza said. You can tell one man apart from another by the way he talks, how he moves, what he says, how he dresses. And what's that add up to? Appearance. Appearance, pure and simple. That was the lesson Luis Coronado had learned in the war. Captain Varela was funny. He used to say, "I didn't come from an ape, like the commies. They say they come from apes and sometimes I think they're right, they do come from apes.

RAFAEL CHIRBES *(1949–) was born in Valencia and studied history in Madrid. He worked as a literary critic for years before turning to other journalistic pursuits as well as to fiction. His first novel,* Mimoun, *was translated into several languages. He has written five other novels, including* La larga marcha *(1996), from which the selection here is taken. "Gran Vía" depicts the dire poverty, pervasive fear, and desperation that characterized post–civil war Madrid in the 1940s.*

But God made me, made me a man and a Spaniard and that's why I have balls, a soul, my country, my flag, and my faith. Maybe he should have made us a little easier to tell apart. Because men and apes look practically the fucking same, if you think about it, especially you, Coronado. You're not a commie, are you?" Coronado had learned that man's mission in life was to separate himself out from the ape. Accentuate the difference. Try his best to ape the ways of polite society and distinguish himself from real apes. That's why before he left home he'd ask his wife to press his trouser creases even more, to iron out a wrinkle in his jacket, which was beginning to apify, to look inhuman, ape-like, with its worn collar and a shine around the pockets and the elbows and cuffs that no one could get rid of, because it sprang from the passage of time, from old age. The uniform was the deciding factor. "You get excited about a present the second you receive it if it's wrapped up in colored paper and not newsprint," Captain Varela would say during his rigorous officer's inspections, "and your uniform is the brightly colored paper that wraps up your bravery and makes it look all pretty and scary at the same time." Approaching the Cine Doré neatly dressed and trying to sell loose cigarettes was quite a job, and when people saw a neatly dressed man, well groomed and well spoken, greeting customers amiably, they were less likely to think that they were buying tobacco salvaged from discarded cigarette butts that his whole family collected at night, that his wife and sister re-rolled with great care; rather, it gave those who could afford to buy cigarettes rather than pick them up off the ground the impression that these were simply goods that—for some strange reason—a gentleman had decided to part with. He had a knack for giving everything he put his hands on a little touch of class, so the cigarettes Luis sold were higher quality than the ones sold by that battalion of badly dressed, foulmouthed apes who set upon anyone leaving the movie house, to shove under their noses—imagine!—what amounted to exactly the same item. Of course, some people get startled when they see a well-dressed man approach, taking him for a cop or the clerk from a store where they haven't paid off their debt, but if you're going to choose your customers you may as well choose good ones. At Gran Vía 44, by way of example, a man he approached with his cigarettes smiled, shook his hand, and though he spurned the cigarettes he chatted for a long while, arranged to meet him another day, and then they met up another afternoon and chatted some more and became friends. After that, whenever they ran into each other they'd go have a coffee, which the other man always paid for, and they'd make vague plans. The gentleman, who said his name was Roberto, said he was going to make Luis a business proposition soon. And not long after that he did. "We should talk about other things. You could do more than sell cigarettes." And he offered him a job delivering merchandise, on a different route and to different customers every day, and the returns were good. He guessed it was penicillin, morphine, cocaine, something like that, something much in demand on the black market at the time. He never once opened those little packets that hardly even weighed a few grams. He thought, if you get caught, it's best not to know anything. Just tell the police exactly what the deal is. That he just makes deliveries, he's not nosy, has no reason to be. With what he earned from that little distribution job, he managed to pay the deposit on the small attic apartment where he lived with his wife and to feed the three children that were born to them—Jesús, the eldest, Laurita, who died of influenza in '46, and Luis junior, the youngest—and it was a shame it all came to an end and that the man from the Gran Vía never showed up again at the bar where they used to meet. Coronado was forced to go back to cigarettes to pay for the abortion of what would have been their fourth child. After all, he still had two other mouths to feed, plus his wife, three, and his sister, four, and his own which was, after all, the biggest, five. Feeding five in Madrid, a city that produced nothing but vice, was no mean feat. The hicks complained about how hard life in the country was and came to the capital in search of opportunity, but it didn't occur to them that Madrid had no orchards, no farmyards, no trout-filled rivers. "Hey, there's no agriculture and no animals here," Coronado would tell the newcomers who wandered around, lost, on Calle Atocha, around La Cebada market, Plaza del Progreso, Carretas, and Puerta del Sol. "And since there's no industry, you have to start your own. You have to industrialize, manage on your own, be your own manager, no other way," he'd say, laughing at his own joke, which was generally way beyond them. "High-quality tobacco, imported, first class," he'd say from inside his jacket, and then add, "Pardon me, sir." And "Can I be of help?" And with an equally elegant, discreet gesture, he'd allow the addressee to glance over the contents of the little wooden box hanging from his neck (on two leather straps, not two strings, which is what the others used) and discover that, besides the cigarettes, there was also a flask of gasoline to soak lighter wicks, plus strips of yellow wick for the lighters, candies, licorice, and a few condoms, which were sort of his firm's luxury item, forbidden goods, available only to the initiated. After all, what man with no money would waste it on rubbers; they cost more than the hookers themselves. "Very good for avoiding diseases," Coronado would explain, looking over his shoulder at the hordes of desperate people dragging themselves miserably through the city streets. The ones who came from nearby towns for a hospital appointment, to get some papers in order, to ask for a recommendation, to look for a job. And the rest. Full-time hookers, part-time hustlers, and small-time jerkers who would swipe your wallet while they were at it, muggers and shoplifters, pickpockets, guys who would do down the first unlucky soul to cross their path, surround him, push, shove, and finger his pocket, and take his wallet in the midst of all the ruckus, and then point at him and shout in unison, "Stop, thief! Stop, thief!" Then they'd leave him in a state of shock, convinced that the police were going to nab him. Coronado wanted nothing to do with them. He was getting by with his family industry—his cigarettes and the doll's clothes his wife and sister sewed from home for a factory over on Blasco de Garay—and he detested the filth that he was only minimally part of—really only infinitesimally—and the language he only ever used in moments of anger, on bad days when he'd drink four glasses of wine and they'd go sour on him. Then he'd lose his composure, damn God to hell, and a stream of obscenities would flow from his mouth. Aside from that, only occasionally had he ever made off with wallets that weren't his, but the people they belonged to were more to blame for the theft than he was, really. They'd leave them in such plain view as they walked out of the movie house or on the tram going up Calle Atocha that only a chump wouldn't make off with them. His only victims had been soldiers, country folk visiting the city, and one night, a businessman from Zaragoza whom he got drunk with and then left near Quevedo, sprawled in a doorway after they'd come out of Las Palmeras. That time he felt no remorse. The other times he had. Playing a dirty trick on some poor wretch who only has a hundred pesetas in his wallet is low, but not bringing home any food for the family is even lower. Besides, this season (he liked those words: season, society) he couldn't stand morons. And things seemed to get worse and worse, rather than better, and now not even his jacket, kind words, the whole blessed kit and caboodle, not even the Virgen del Carmen helped him sell anything. As if the whole country, instead of escaping from a war, was running headlong toward another. In Madrid there were more and more desperate souls, people on the run, thinking they'd find refuge right in the country's biggest wasteland. Madrid, with no orchards, no corrals, no trout-filled rivers. Ever since the day he took the businessman's wallet (which held less than the man's appearance and conversation had led him to expect), Coronado hadn't gone back to Las Palmeras, and he felt uneasy walking down Gran Vía even though the guy was already so drunk and so far gone when they met that he didn't think he'd ever recognize him, even if they bumped right into each other. Madrid was a city that swallowed people up, a huge voracious beast.

Translated by Lisa Dillman

Beatriz Comes Home

Lucía Etxebarria

SIX HOURS ON A TRAIN to Victoria Station. Transfer there to the Gatwick Express, which leaves me at the airport. I only have one suitcase, because everything I managed to accumulate over the last four years (clothes, books, records . . .) I left at Cat's. I might go back in September, even if it's just to pack up my things and send them to Madrid. But I don't want to think about that now: about the wide-eyed look Cat gave me when I tried to explain how much I missed home, about the silent protest I read in her expression, about my own feelings of guilt at not including her in my plans, not suggesting that we both—rather than just me—move to Madrid. Give

---

LUCÍA ETXEBARRIA *(1966–) is a novelist, poet, essayist, and scriptwriter. She holds a doctorate from the University of Aberdeen, Scotland, where she also taught scriptwriting. She considers herself a typical Sagittarius rising—a born traveler with no fixed residence. "Beatriz Comes Home," an excerpt from the novel* Beatriz y los cuerpos celestes, *which won the Nadal Prize in 1998, recounts the conflicting emotions of a young woman who has just graduated from college and left her girlfriend in Scotland to return to her parents' house in Madrid after a four-year absence.*

me some time, I said. Let me go home for a few months, and then I'll decide.

A one-hour wait at Gatwick spent browsing the sale items at the Body Shop in the duty-free. I stop at a bottle of Activist, Caitlin's cologne, a men's fragrance that's supposed to smell like Chanel's Antaneus. I spritz a cloud of perfume onto the back of my hand and suddenly conjure up the image of Caitlin's lithe body, cuddling up to my back, her smooth, supple skin touching mine. In a fit of sentimentality, I buy the bottle (seven pounds) and suddenly, out of the blue, realize that I don't have a single photo of her in my wallet or my bag, and that over the next two months, or however long, I will only be able to remember her by that smell.

On the plane I'm seated next to an insufferable couple. Highlighted hair and Fiorucci pants for her. Ray Bans and striped shirt for him. Holding hands. They spent a dreamy weekend buying name brands and taking pictures of Big Ben. I've always wondered why people like that bother with photos when they could just buy postcards. Why this desire to immortalize buildings that will surely outlive them?

Someone ought to come up with some kind of seat-assignment compatibility system for airlines. You'd fill out a form when you booked your ticket and turn it in with your boarding card. Age, favorite bands, what paper you read. Three things you'd take to a desert island. Do you travel alone? Believe in collective art? Eat meat? Have kids? Want to have them? Have you ever had group sex? What do you think of Prince Charles? Cindy Crawford? k.d. lang? Favorite designer? Perfume? Concept artist? Then a computer would tabulate your answers with the rest of the passengers' to come up with the seating plan.

If this system were enforced, the airline would have sat this darling little couple by a spinster who taught English, whereas I would have been put next to a couple of queers or a pretty boy who was going to Madrid to teach English at some language academy and get over his girlfriend. The charming couple's chatter becomes unbearable, slipping into my brain despite my efforts to concentrate on my reading. He takes great delight in giving her a rundown of London trivia doubtlessly picked up from an Anaya travel guide. She responds with comments that lead me to suspect she has yet to read a book in her life, even an Anaya travel guide. I lean over my book and don't raise my head again except for the fifteen minutes I spend picking listlessly at the plastic food the flight attendant serves on a tray made of the same.

Airport arrival. As soon as I walk through the glass doors dividing the passengers-only area from the greeting area, I can make out my mother's silhouette: she's in black from head to toe. Her short, blond hair and impeccably tailored suit give her a Marlene Dietrich air, at least from a distance. But the impression fades as I approach her. Her wrinkles belie the fact that she's too old to play the femme fatale, though she's still got a fantastic body for someone about to turn sixty. When she sees me, she hugs me with so much fervor that I stiffen up, not knowing how to respond appropriately. I don't even know why I feel strange. Guilt is like an iceberg: most of it lies below the surface.

We take a taxi. She gives the driver the address, checks herself in the rearview mirror and runs her fingers through her hair coquettishly. Then she turns back to face me. Her smell, the same scent she's been wearing for years—because my fickle mother, who changes her wardrobe every year and the upholstery on her easy chairs every three, is only faithful to her husband, her God, and her perfume—bathes me in a familiar atmosphere, and a wave of retrospective affection wells up inside me in spite of myself. She explains, though I didn't ask, that my father didn't come because he was feeling a little under the weather; and in a whisper designed, I suppose, to rob the taxi driver of this confidential information that he, I am sure, is not the least bit interested in, she informs me that lately my father is not the man he once was. I didn't want to tell you over the phone, or in a letter, she informs me, but there's a good chance they'll have to operate on him soon. The doctors think he needs a bypass. I don't say anything. I have no idea what a bypass is.

Next we turn to her standard thesis, the single-subject speech she's been giving for years now: my looks. Actually, I am surprised it has taken her this long to work around to it. I'm too thin, she thinks, and hair this short doesn't look good on me. Why do I insist on cropping it all off this way? And do I really have to wear these well-digger boots all the time? They're so unfeminine. Silently, I repeat the magic words: *you're not responsible for my life. I'm not responsible for your life.* And I try to convince myself that the spell really works so I don't get dragged back down into that awful mix of resentment and wretched self-pity that drowned me for years. I believe in magic, in the power of words, in life-saving mantras. If I didn't, I wouldn't read. So I try to treat her singsong voice like background noise, like rainfall, and

I stare out the window at the city that awaits me. Horrible concrete and cement buildings, one after the other, like posts nailed onto the parched yellow ground. The sky is white rather than blue. It's true that the sunshine brightens everything—your spirits and the view—but this prospect, in contrast with my memory of Edinburgh—elegant stone buildings, humid skies, plants that climbed walls and covered parks—seems poor and dry, unpromising, a bad omen.

The closer to the city we get, the more intense the feeling becomes. Suddenly, I realize that Madrid is dirty, gray, poorly planned, lacking in personality. I can't detect the hand of an architect in any building; no street seems to have a story to tell. What's going on here? Isn't this the same city I missed so brokenheartedly over the last four years?

The taxi stops in front of our door. Until today I had never realized what an ugly building it is: grimy, solemn, poorly lit. Riding up in the decrepit elevator—a vestige of better times when the pulley system must have been the latest scream in technology—has become a game of Russian roulette, and the shrill creaks and groans it emits as it sets off call to mind all manner of imminent catastrophes.

Home is the same as when I left it, but dustier. The living room looks like it's from another century. Walls covered with tapestries, walnut armchairs with velvet upholstery, bronze lamps with glass tulips, a huge armoire with a modernist mirror. When I lived here, I never realized they were all genuine antique pieces. The light filtering through the heavy velvet curtains plays on the edges of the furniture, creating shadows that give the room an even creepier look, if that's possible. I walk through the room dragging my suitcase as if it were a cadaver and collecting, unawares, little crumbs of my childhood, scattered throughout the corners of my old home.

My room, I realize now for the first time, is also too ornate. All the furniture is solid walnut, and there are wood soffits. The crest on the bed's headboard matches the dresser and the center of the armoire. Before, when I still lived here, I couldn't appreciate the sturdiness of the furniture, the veneer of time on the wood, its character, its resounding beauty, its value. Now I admire it, having spent years sleeping on a cheap stuffed mattress with no springs, resting precariously on a wooden frame that Cat herself had made. But though I admire the furniture's beauty, it isn't comforting or welcoming, not at all. The bed is perfectly made, and my mother has covered it with an immaculate white bedspread. You can tell by the monastic air in the room that no one has slept here for a while. My books are still piled on the shelves, but otherwise there are no traces of my presence. When I lived here there were papers scattered on the desk, photos thumbtacked to the wall, posters hanging; now the walls have been repainted white, and they are bare, devoid of any of my remnants, without personality.

My father is sleeping, my mother informs me, but I can say hi to him at lunch. It would be best, she thinks, if I went and had a shower and got dressed. You must be exhausted after your flight, honey. Indeed, I am exhausted.

The luxuries of home don't cease to surprise me, all those marvels that I had never, until now, picked up on. The shower, for instance. The water stays at a constant temperature, rather than suddenly going cold and freezing you to death or scalding you without warning. The water pressure is strong, and a solid, energetic stream—torrents of water—cascades over me. Nothing like that piddling little trickle at Cat's, that pathetic shower that we improvised by attaching two ends of a Y-shaped rubber hose to the hot and cold faucets, since old houses in Scotland don't have showers, just bathtubs.

I step out of the shower and wrap myself in a huge terry cloth towel that smells clean and fresh, like Mimosín fabric softener. I turn and face the shadow of my reflection in the misty mirror. I wipe off the steam with the back of my wrist and see myself more clearly. I'm thin. Skinny, as my mother would say. My hip bones stick out so far that it's easy to imagine my skeleton. I cover my breasts with my hands and cross one leg in front of the other. I'm happy to report that my body is like an adolescent's, like a Calvin Klein model's.

I remember one night in Edinburgh, on the dance floor at Cream. Dancing among the moving shadows of other bodies dancing with me, surrounding me, I collided with an apparition, exposed suddenly by the spotlight that came to rest on her. A very thin girl, nodding her head back and forth in time to the music. Her short hair fell like a golden curtain over her eyes. She was wearing a very tight T-shirt that showed her pierced bellybutton—the epicenter of her washboard stomach—and proclaimed *Monogamy is unnatural* across her flat chest. Miraculously frozen in time, she had managed to combine that fleeting moment when childhood and adolescence blend into one, and she stood in a motionless present, her own territory, oblivious to the slow passage of time and the inevitable deterioration it brings. It was the most erotic image I'd ever seen in my life. Now I look in the mirror and realize how much that stranger and I resemble one another, eternal adolescents, androgynous bodies, residency permits in never-never land with no expiration date.

I don't know if I'll always be like this, but I do remember that there was a time, back when I first became a teenager, when I voluntarily starved myself, those years when I hardly ate at all. Food made me nauseated; rejecting it filled me with pleasure. My ribs were hooks, my spine a knife and my hunger a shield, the only weapons I had to fight back against the frivolities that stuck to my body like ticks each time I took a misplaced step toward the world of womanhood. Fasting was a prolonged resistance to change, the only way I could think of to keep the dignity I possessed as a girl and would lose as a woman. I didn't want to be a woman. I chose not to limit my future decisions to little things and not to let others decide the big ones for me. I chose not to belong to the legion of resigned second-class citizens. I chose not to be like my mother. The wasted body I see before me is the result of a conscious decision, of an absurd trial of strength.

I barely have time to get dressed before my mother tells me lunch is ready. And in the dining room, finally, I see my father, who drags his feet across the carpet in order to greet me. His appearance shocks me. He looks twenty years older than the last time I saw him. He's lost a ton of weight, his gray hair is thinning at the temples, and a million tiny wrinkles line his forehead. He looks like a Munch painting. I almost can't recognize the once dashing, good-looking, sixty-something gentleman. His pristine blue eyes, still shining with their own light, are his only alluring feature intact from those days. We give each other a quick, restrained hug before sitting down to eat. When he asks me how I am, I note a change in his voice: it's lost its deep tones and seems to restrict its register to a kind of feeble croakiness, a monotonous, laryngitic sound.

During the course of the meal we go over the hackneyed questions—Did I have a good flight? Am I tired? Have I thought about what I'm going to do now that I have a college degree?—while the midday sun, which filters in through the blinds that are lowered in an attempt to keep down the heat, projects strange shadows on the walls. The weight of the memories floating through the house threatens to flatten me against the table. And I don't know if I'm all that happy to be back.

Translated by Lisa Dillman

Let the Passengers Off

José Ferrer Bermejo

SURPRISINGLY, he finds himself once again on the empty platform and, in shock, sits down on one of the benches. He tries to compose himself by thinking things over; he lights a cigarette deliberately and breathes deeply the warm air from the tunnels. He notices the big ads on the opposite platform: a brand of shoes, an airline, a drink. He also observes the chocolate and chewing gum vending machines, the benches, the wastepaper bins. . . . In the small glass office, a sleepy worker leafs through a newspaper at the table. It's obvious: it was a simple error, a series of silly mistakes, something that could happen to any city dweller. Taking hungry drags on his cigarette he reconstructs the facts: he took the metro at Argüelles at approximately half past six; after work he'd spent a little time buying some cotton handkerchiefs in the big depart-

JOSÉ FERRER BERMEJO *was born in Alcalá de Henares and has lived most of his life in central Madrid. After studying history, teacher training, and navigation, he worked as a merchant marine for several years. He now works for the post office in Madrid. Bermejo has published five novels and three books of short stories. "Let the Passengers Off" comes from his 1982 collection,* Incidente en Atocha.

ment store on the corner of Calle Princesa and Calle Alberto Aguilera and was in a hurry to get to his date; he went down to the platform, the Sol train arrived normally, and the stations passed by without any mishap—Ventura Rodríguez, Plaza de España, Callao, Sol. When the doors opened he'd got out quite calmly, taking care as always not to put his foot between the coach and the platform; he then went into the Exit to Mayor passageway, where he clearly remembers throwing a coin into the cap of a young man who was sitting on the ground playing a guitar; a few paces past the busker a gypsy woman cradling a sleeping child stretched out her hand for money, which he gave gladly and with dignity, as was his custom; and after a few twists and turns and going up and down some stairs he found himself on the same platform he'd just left. From the opposite platform and near the shoe ad, a bespectacled woman observed him carefully, and he hastily studied the metro map behind him to hide his embarrassment. But he immediately regained his composure, because after all anyone can slip up and he was in a hurry, a real hurry, to get to his date; so off he went again toward Mayor, passed the gypsy woman who was still begging, turned, went down, came up. . . . A chill ran through him when he again saw the same ads for the shoes, the airline, and the drink, the same benches, the same chocolate and gum vending machines, the same worker reading the newspaper in his office, and the same bespectacled woman watching him with growing curiosity.

It's this sudden chill running down his spine that has made him sit down on the bench and light a cigarette in order to examine the situation carefully. There are days when your head feels crazy and things like this happen, especially if you consider certain problems, all the things there are to think about, and, above all, a very important date for which he has been conditioning his life for some time now. Rashness and perhaps nerves too have played a nasty trick on him which, as the platform gradually fills up with passengers, he now finds slightly funny. That must be it; that's all there is to it. It's only as important as you make it—anyone can make a mistake, even if they've been traveling on the metro all their lives.

Suddenly a distant rumble can be heard, gradually drawing nearer, until a train explodes into view to his left, on the opposite track; it screeches to a halt, opens its doors, and after a few seconds whistles and is off toward Moncloa. The bespectacled woman is still watching him through a window until the train disappears into the blackness of the tunnel. Another train arrives to his right, and he looks at but doesn't read the words written above each door: LET THE PASSENGERS OFF. He finishes his cigarette and, sighing, tells himself that all this has been simply a huge load of nonsense.

But now he has to hurry—he cannot delay any longer if he wants to be on time for his date. He picks up his packet of cotton handkerchiefs and again goes into the Exit to Mayor passageway; he smiles with pleasure when he hears the notes of the young guitarist and the gypsy's incoherent words as she begs, he turns a couple of corners, crosses the paths of people moving quickly and nervously, goes down some stairs, up some others, and emerges on the same platform, with the shoes, the planes, the benches, and the worker, like a statue, reading his newspaper.

Now he's stopped smiling.

He feels a strange rage inside his body, clenches his teeth, and would like to bang his head against the wall. This is stupid, irritating, especially now that he's in a hurry, such a terrible, terrible hurry. Like a caged lion, he paces the length of the platform, curses under his breath, not caring that people look askance at him (to hell with them!). He tosses his packet of handkerchiefs (which now seems the most absurd package in the world) into a wastepaper bin and in a fury rashly forsakes all the possible solutions suggested by his rational instinct for survival: follow someone? Ah! Everyone is going somewhere, but no one is going where he wants to go, to his most important date ever, jeopardized now by an idiotic incident that no longer strikes him as remotely amusing. Should he ask for help, from some worker perhaps? Yes, that would be a fine thing! So they could take him for some kind of idiot or illiterate! Isn't the sign—blue letters on a white background—Exit to Mayor—perfectly clear? Ask for directions, he who'd used the metro all his life, since he was a boy? Ask, he who knows every line by heart and the name of every station? Like hell! Right now he will come out on the street in the Puerta del Sol, behind the newspaper kiosk, and see to his left the government security headquarters, and opposite it Calle Mayor, and farther on the café where his date is waiting for him, impatiently by now, where he'll order a stiff drink to forget this intolerable episode that's been going on for far too long. It's those idiotic architects or engineers or whatever the hell they're called who are to blame, making the metro an impenetrable maze where even the smartest guy could get lost. Like a whirlwind he rushes into the passageway where the boy is still playing (he hardly notices the gypsy has disappeared), turns a couple of times, bumps into everyone who crosses his path, goes down some stairs, up others, and round and round again. . . .

Suddenly everything seems very quiet to him. Even the train that comes whistling out of the black cave to his right seems to arrive in slow motion; it opens its doors very slowly, and passengers come and go as if floating. The gypsy who was begging earlier in the passageway is there now, at the end of the platform, taking the packet of handkerchiefs out of the wastepaper bin where he'd thrown them, smiling and disappearing. The train whistles and closes its doors, leaves; as it rumbles off, he stares yet again, stiff as a dummy, at the words written over the doors that make a sort of endless reel, OFFLETTHEPASSENGERSOFFLETTHEPASSENGERSOFF. A growing anguish gets the better of him; the walls, the ground, the curved ceiling and dangling cables, the rails below, gleaming against the greasy dirt of the cement and sleepers, seem oppressive. He looks around with the envy of the condemned man who sees everyone as privileged and able to enjoy something he is about to lose; everyone is going somewhere, people come and go, but he is there still, in the same place he was a few minutes ago, still scrutinizing the adverts, the benches, the vending machines, the worker still reading—how can it be!—the newspaper in the same posture. A knot in his throat brings tears to his eyes, and now he wishes he'd kept at least one of the handkerchiefs he'd bought; but the gypsy with the strange smile and the sleeping child wrapped in her colorful shawl has taken them all.

Mechanically, like a horse on a fairground carousel, he turns to start on his path again, entering the Exit to Mayor passageway. The guitarist is there, keeping faith with his niche in the cosmos. Oddly, he doesn't have the look of a rebel without a cause or a hobo adventurer: he is a young man with not very long hair, wearing clean shoes and polyester trousers. He plays the guitar very well, performing conscientiously, without lifting his head from the frets, a fairground, gypsy style of music, whose rhythm the frustrated passenger follows while turning a couple of corners, concentrating only on going down some stairs, up others, and appearing like a dummy on the same eternal platform: adverts for planes, shoes, and drinks; benches, wastepaper bins, and gum vending machines; a worker reading a newspaper; people. A melody plays behind him in the passageway, and at the end, to his right, emerging from the dark tunnel like a furious dragon, there is yet another train with twin headlights that spark off a strange attraction, hypnotize like a mysterious magnet, and make him dance a few steps toward the platform's edge.

Translated by John McCarthy

Sex, Food, and the Family

Angela Vallvey

"OH, GOD. OH, GOD!" My grandmother is chewing cautiously. She always looks as if she were trying to eat very carefully just in case she should find any foreign bodies in her food; in fact, it's because her false teeth aren't of quite the same high quality as Aunt Mary's.

"For heaven's sake, Grandma, now what's wrong with you?" Carmina is sitting next to her and reluctantly puts her fork down beside her plate. She turns her large, round head to meet Grandma's gaze.

When she sees that the ruminative process is continuing normally, she relaxes her facial muscles and picks up her fork again.

"Granny, stop frightening us."

"To do that she'd have to be born again, with a different

ANGELA VALLVEY *(Ciudad Real, 1964–) won the Nadal Prize for Fiction in 2002. She lives between Geneva and Getafe. This extract is from her satirical, Almodóvaresque novel,* Hunting the Last Wild Man *(1999), which has been translated into English, French, and Italian. She has also published children's fiction and poetry and won the Jaén Prize for Poetry in 1998.*

face," comments Aunt Mary, to my grandmother's complete indifference.

"I wasn't talking about the food," my grandmother says, looking at my sister Carmina. "It's just that last night I dreamed that they came to take away the only thing a woman my age has left."

"What's that, then?"

"Her happy memories."

I laugh, and my niece Paula looks at me with wide, questioning eyes. That girl is so damned serious.

"I still feel as if I was in that dream. I'm starting to feel breathless . . . Ela, I can't eat any more of this . . . this . . . whatever it is. Bring me some ham," my grandmother orders.

"There isn't any. I used up the leftovers in the stew."

"Oh well, never mind, I've had enough anyway."

"Eat a bit more, Mama."

"I don't feel like it."

I've heard it said that in order to know how someone makes love, you just have to watch how they eat. I've heard it said that people have the same manners eating as they do copulating; the same style, shall we say. I begin to study my family carefully. There are nine women round the table, a load of greedy pigs with their chairs pulled up to the trough, all brandishing their knives and forks with varying degrees of skill and incompetence. I look at my own hands. I haven't even been able to touch my knife because I get the shivers just thinking about all the things one could do with a sharp instrument. The things that could be done to my fair head with one of those cheap household knives. The knives at home are all blunt because, since Carmina is a butcher,

Mama always brings the meat home perfectly filleted, sliced, or cut up. We don't need any stupid jack knives with a point on them like D'Artagnan's dagger. The most difficult thing we have to do is slice open watermelons, and if they prove stubborn, Carmina disembowels them by smashing them down on the table and we eat them like that. Nevertheless, even a blunt knife that has never been sharpened is still a knife. And right now there must be at least two unscrupulous men on my trail, with, instead of teeth, knives as long as the motorway to Andalusia. Really. Almost certainly.

The result is that I don't eat, I've no appetite. Consequently, we might say that I am also anorexic in bed, as far as sex is concerned.

Beside me is Paula, my niece. She has the receding chin and frightened face of a little mouse. She is so thin you can count her bones. Her eyes are as big and round as the salad bowl and are dirty blue in color. Her mouth is stuffed with frozen hake, but she can't swallow. Then again, she is only five years old. It's hard to know what she'll be like in bed when she's older.

Then there's Gádor, sitting on the other side of her daughter. I imagine that the new pregnancy has left her slightly traumatized. I watch her pick up a piece of vegetable, put it eagerly in her mouth, then start fiddling with her fork and gazing with disgust at the stew on her plate.

My grandmother hardly eats a thing, apart from ham or, very occasionally, a sandwich made from thin slices of bread and pork loin; she costs us less to feed than a stuffed canary. One day, I asked her, "Are you following some kind of special regime, Grandma?" and without even glancing up, she said, "Regime? The only regime I ever followed, and then only a bit, at the start, was the Franco regime. . . . And look what happened to that. Don't talk to me about regimes. A lot of modern nonsense."

Beside her, Carmina is devouring her food as if, rather than just eating the vegetables, she wanted to hurt them, to vent her spleen on them. I regard her with interest. She spears a Brussels sprout with her fork and carries it to her mouth, then, before she has had time even to begin to chew, she spears some beans and puts those in her mouth too, along with a little pile of peas, two bits of fried ham, some carrots and onion . . . and only on the sixth mouthful does she allow herself to chew and momentarily close her mouth. She's voracious. That's Carmina for you. If she fell over, she'd bounce. I dread to think what she's like in bed. I'm too much of a prude to think everything I could think about Carmina if I wanted to.

My mother eats resignedly. I blush and move on.

Ah, Aunt Mary. What a sublime sight. Something dribbles out of the corner of her mouth and she greedily licks it up. She takes a large swig of sherry and makes a few pathetic attempts to reach the bread basket, meanwhile shooting furious glances at us all, hoping that someone will help her without her having to ask. She snorts when Bely passes her the bread. She eats too much, but she doesn't put on weight, and when she goes to the loo, she leaves behind her turds the size of a small child. I fear that she will live a very long time.

Bely eats slowly, but without pauses or interruptions, as if she were immensely patient and determined to get to the end regardless of what awaits her there.

And Brandy is a sight to behold; she has transformed the

act of chewing into an art form. The way she chews her food is almost lascivious, or, rather, it's totally lascivious, perhaps because she's imagining sharing the table with eight Canadian lumberjacks, which we most certainly are not. Before she got married, Gádor said to me one night that Brandy pulled more men than anyone she knew. "What does she put behind her ears, Essence of Cunt?" she said rather irritably. I suppose that for Gádor, who lives by the slogan "Liberty, Equality, Maternity," it must be very hard to accept that there are women like Brandy in the world.

For her part, Brandy knew—as we all did—that when Gádor got married, and despite being twenty years old, she had had no previous sexual experience; she had always been the kind of unvanquished virgin you see at the Parthenon in Athens, only a flesh-and-blood variety of very little brain. So that when Brandy went to congratulate her, once the wedding ceremony was over, if the bawling choirboys at the parish church merit the name "ceremony," instead of saying, "Congratulations, little sister," she whispered in her ear, "You know what they say, a cock in the hand . . ." and Gádor burst out crying all over my freshly ironed pink organdie collar, whining, "How could she, the whore, the slut? How could she . . ."

I've lost my appetite completely now. We're like some perverse, gastronomic version of *Little Women*.

"May one know why you're pulling that face?" Mama asks me while she dabs carelessly at her mouth, chin, throat, and—very, very nearly—the cleavage of her flowery bosom.

As soon as they married, Victor and Gádor decided to

opt for family planning and bought some fluorescent condoms off an African selling them in the street market that were about as impermeable as a tea bag; she became pregnant, acquired loads of dark stretch marks all over her breasts and, after giving birth to Paula, assured me that it had been the longest, most unpleasant experience she had ever been through. "Absolutely bloody awful," she told me, as she was tenderly covering up her little girl, asleep in a wicker basket decorated with some cotton fabric printed with little red bears, each one of whom had the charming smile of a psychopath stamped on its little purple snout. "When I was five months gone and realized that what goes in must come out, I didn't sleep a wink until the pregnancy was over, because it's a real shock, you know. It's not just like putting in a Tampax and then taking it out again, and God knows I found it hard enough learning how to use a Tampax," she told me.

And yet during her first year of marriage, Gádor seemed contented enough. Ignorance is a marvelous antidote to common sense. One day she asked Brandy and me what she should give her beloved husband for their wedding anniversary. "Well," said Brandy, while she was applying some aubergine-colored dye—like coagulated blood—to Gádor's scalp, "in my experience, men are always in need of two things: socks and fellatio." "Fellawhat?" Gádor looked up and a drop of the disgusting gloop ran along her right eyebrow. "It comes from Latin, idiot. Languages never were your strong point, were they? Socks will do fine," replied Brandy. After that, Gádor and I went to the local library, and I checked out Dr. López Ibor's *Sexual Encyclopedia* for her, because, at the time, I myself couldn't give her an entirely accurate technical description of what was involved. I had my own ideas on the subject, but I never was much good at Latin and indeed discovered that I was completely on the wrong track, and had got the wrong terminology and even the wrong body parts. From then on, Gádor improved her family planning with, for a few years, considerable success, until eight months ago. One must study constantly in order not to forget what one already knows.

Translated by Margaret Jull Costa

No Reply

Agustín Cerezales

WHAT WAS INÉS PEREIRA DOING, selling bootleg cassettes in the middle of Calle Preciados on a wet April afternoon, alone under a large fisherman's umbrella, her feet resting on the trestle of her folding chair, so they wouldn't get soaked in the murky deluge descending from the Plaza Callao?

In flight from a mid-fifteenth-century convent, a pallid melomane, radiating serene intelligence from lips and eyes, she seemed, with her white skin, a blatant historical error in this turbulent century of ours.

But categorical statements are fungible: the epitome of adolescence, Inés was at the same time impossible to define. As far as her intelligence, apparent or real, is concerned, suffice it to say just one thing: if in childhood intelligence and innocence are unhappy bedfellows, received wisdom

AGUSTÍN CEREZALES *(Madrid, ca. 1956–) has worked as a journalist, translator, painter and decorator, and screenplay writer, among other things, and is the son of the late novelist Carmen Martín Gaite. This chronicle of the swinging Madrid of the 1980s comes from his collection of novellas,* Perros verdes *(1989), a gallery of enigmatic Almodovarian women.*

has it that with age they divorce. However—and here it gets complicated—Inés continued believing what she believed, saying what she said, and thinking what she thought, alarmingly devoid of the usual adult duplicity. What was it that Inés believed, said, thought? For one thing, that she was a punk.

Slight, with a very soft complexion and narrow jawline; full-lipped, rather snub-nosed, and hazel-eyed: her look was full, pristine as autumn. An erotic creature, then, whose appearance might bore the vulgar yet excite the sensitive soul. Inés, though—and this is what mattered to her—was above all a punk. A punk! Dressed so discreetly, with her pleated skirt, braids, and schoolgirl air, who would have thought it? Anyway, as Eduardo argued, how could she be a punk? Punks had been dead and buried for years, embalmed on the covers of magazines. Where were the piercings, the safety-pinned ears, the colored hair, and leather trousers? No, she couldn't be a punk. But she was, nevertheless. And she didn't feel like proving it to anyone. Her own personal conviction sufficed, complete with principles and a style of behavior that made explanations unnecessary. And if she didn't think that way, she at least acted accordingly.

There was no end to the questions. Why had she escaped from Braga, her hometown? To evade definition? Or perhaps just for a change of century, out of a thirst for adventure?

The fact is that dressed thus she was a schoolgirl who never aroused suspicions. The police didn't ask to see her I.D. card, though everyday they insisted on seeing those of her friends, clad in black with Nazi badges on their backsides. It was an issue that riled some of the group. But Inés was no pushover. She knew only too well that she was the punk of punks, had the code down to a T, and her singularity was in fact the shortest path to difference, the goal pursued in every denial of convention.

In addition to this stubborn desire to be herself—or more than herself—Inés had other idiosyncrasies. The first and most striking of these was her love of the lollipop. She always had one in her mouth and several in her pockets, giving her sugar-coated rainbow lips an even more childish air, if that's possible. She only had to smile and, paradoxically, her lolly habit allowed her to emulate the black teeth of any junkie or speed freak who might dispute her asphalt kingdom.

Another of Inés's specialities was cooking. She combined innate Portuguese savoir-faire and passion for a fiery art. She cooked with her eyes: normally she neither tasted nor ate her stews. She much preferred the sweets that numbed her palate but not her sight, which was all she needed to know how things were going.

Just as a day's temperature and humidity are reflected in the color and texture of the most ordinary slab of concrete, faithfully mirroring what is happening in the atmosphere, in her opinion the difference between insipid and spicy was equally an optical question, a visible texturing: all substances interact, and spices are certainly not the least powerful of these. Vegetables change color on contact with them, retain or exude juices, as do meats. Similar paradigms warn whether something is raw or cooked, sweet or sour, bland or salty. But what of rice, pastas, bread? How to read their intrinsic truths?

That was another of her secrets, and secrets in fact constituted one of her main sources of pleasure. That's why nobody—except Eduardo—knew precisely where she was from, what she was looking for, or even what she really understood by the word "punk."

Those who loved Inés—and during that long stormy summer there were more than a few—couldn't explain either what it was that made her an exceptional creature.

"Love," on the other hand, she wouldn't allow into her vocabulary. None of her suitors ever got a kiss or caress out of her, but neither were they rejected or treated unkindly. A magnetic shield seemed to separate her from the world. Inés's expression and the light of her eyes held an eternal yes, but her yes was like the bullfighter's cape, a tense, undulating illusion facing the hollow geometry of silence.

No doubt about it: Inés alone was mistress of herself, only she knew where she would lavish the deep tenderness constantly flickering in her mischievous child's eyes. Eduardo himself knew that he knew nothing, which was quite true: he couldn't even divine how Inés had already given her heart.

Calle Preciados was a river whose fluctuating flow barely swirled around the stall of pirated tapes and punk knick-knacks that Inés looked after when Ricardo and Elena went off to lunch.

Inés lived these moments with special intensity. The first thing she'd do when left alone was take out the little mirror they had for the customers and fix her hair. Then, as though it were the last thing on her mind, flushed with love, she would look out for him. And every day he would appear at a quarter to two without fail, coming wearily around the corner with his crumpled briefcase and charming spectacles.

She loved him. He awoke in her an odd feeling, a kind of sincere, moving admiration. It was truly a habitual feeling by now, inspired by the same type of man: that humble, unknown man, whose shoulders bear, though no one notices, the entire terrible burden of that fearsome brew we call society. People you can't really call proletarian, because they're not workers or sons of the soil, but who don't fit into the middle classes either, despite their roots being there. As a rule, their lives unfold along narrow physical and moral grooves. In the former they share, perhaps, something of the proletariat; in the latter, something of the bourgeoisie. What is their own, then, remains their mysterious spiritual condition.

Although not defined by their occupations, it so happens they are often ticket collectors, commercial reps for unfashionable goods, box-office clerks, ushers—apparently superfluous jobs that anyone could do without too much effort, but that in reality fulfill a crucial mission, the importance of that escapes them, though cynics and lovers may have an inkling.

They are totally devoid of ambition and, consequently, of frustration. They occupy their positions without thinking of other possibilities or dreaming of anything better. If they have any nostalgia, it is locked in the depths of their souls. They can be seen at daybreak turning up punctually for work, and then at nightfall returning, gray and invisible, immersed in asphalt humility, at one with their smoky sadness. It is a humility that, like a muffler, protects them from cold and indiscretion.

Inés loved him. She loved him as she loved all his kind, but in this case with such intensity that one might call it rapture. She loved his imagined childhood, his strangely obedient, simple youth, his maturing right on time. . . . She loved his thick jersey and the engraved ring on his middle finger, next to the wedding ring; she loved his hairy, swollen fingers. She loved his worn-out woven shoes, molded to his feet's idiosyncrasies; his darned socks; his tortoiseshell glasses, misted with use; the trousers let out as his waistline expanded; his methodically tired gait, doubled under the weight of time; his indeterminate age; his constancy; his patience; his fidelity. . . .

She imagined his home: the round table over a brazier, a sick wife, a cheeky child. And the tears came to her eyes. She enjoyed her sadness alone, her misplaced yearning to redeem him. To all this she added, like a magic veneer, keen curiosity: she would have liked to know what mysterious reasoning sustained this man, what it was that separated him from suicide, ambition, glory, what caused him to see in slavery and poverty a life worthy of being lived.

When Inés realized that her man went by each day at the same time, taking the same route, she arranged to swap shifts with Ricardo and Elena, and devoted herself wholly to the exciting task of following Juan Rodríguez and spying on his every movement.

Juan always ate in the same tavern in Calle Peligros and worked in the accounts department of a rope warehouse in an alleyway off Calle Jacometrezo. He was a sprightly walker, and Inés was surprised by his nimble short legs and the elegance with which he sidestepped the throng in the narrow little streets and continually disappeared from sight.

Inés wasted no time in becoming a regular at Casa Julián herself and often sat at the same table as her loved one, whose meal was always the same: broth, a steak, and salad. The only occasional change was fried eggs instead of the steak. The girl was amazed by his lack of curiosity about other dishes, although she was somewhat similar and kept mostly to tomatoes and cheese.

Inés interrogated him relentlessly and this he accepted with good humor, although he was always sparing in his answers. He smiled at her Portuguese accent, which, lovingly adapted to Spanish, banished the hardness of both languages. Inés wanted to know everything, was interested in the smallest detail, but hardly ever in the whys and wherefores. Hers was a restless rather than intrusive curiosity. Don Juan ate at the same place every day, in fact, but only in summer, when he worked an intensive shift (his intensive shift meant he had an hour less for lunch and left work at seven rather than eight in the evening). In winter he ate at home with his wife. His wife wasn't a bad cook. No, she wasn't eating alone now, she was away on holiday. In Panticosa, at a spa: she had kidney trouble. She used to go with their son, Juanito, but now the boy wanted to do his own thing, so she was travelling with a niece. Juanito didn't spend the summer in Madrid either. He was off at the seaside, working as a waiter, or at least that's what he said.

"Ah . . ."

Inés drank in all the information from Don Juan's lips as if it were the Holy Gospel, thoroughly charmed, and her eyes opened wide so as not to miss a thing.

"So your name's Juan Rodríguez. There are lots of Rodrigues in my country too, but without the 'z'."

"My name's Rodríguez but I'm not on the 'razzle.' Do you have the same expression in Portugal?"

Don Juan, who treated her warmly, never asked her any but this kind of perfectly innocuous question. There's no doubt it was less disturbing for him to find quite normal the presence of this little Portuguese girl with her lollipops and braids, selling cassettes and bracelets on the street. Inés was a little put out by his lack of curiosity, but she consoled herself with the thought that he was just being considerate.

One day Don Juan took a packet of sweets out of his pocket. They were better quality than the ones she usually ate, contained less sugar, and maybe, he explained, even contained some nourishment. It was, on the face of it, a fatherly gesture, but Inés interpreted it in her own way. To her it was very clear that at last she was starting to live inside Don Juan, inhabiting him and making him hers. And this had a name, a name her lips knew only inside for the moment but very soon must kiss his eyes and mouth, skin and ears.

She decided from then on she would eat only Paco sweets, like the ones Don Juan had given her, unwittingly beginning the sweetest and craziest of liaisons.

Inés would have confided everything to Eduardo, as secrets, after all, are for sharing. She wouldn't have told him everything exactly, of course, but by telling him a little, the rest would have been understood. But it rained that day. A torrential downpour, not unusual in Madrid in the middle of August. And Inés, who greeted the downpour as an echo or expression of her own inner turmoil, sat there under the black fisherman's umbrella that Ricardo used to protect himself against the relentless sun.

The hours passed; no one was about; the rain fell, flooding the entire province. The governor didn't know whether he'd have to swim out of his office; there were television reports of the president flying over the affected areas, and for Inés the storm was but an emanation of her love, an explosion of her disquiet.

The next day she had a temperature. She'd slept at the usual place, in the abandoned hangar that was the Pumpi gang's headquarters, lying in a draft with wet hair, in an ecstasy of pain and loneliness.

Eduardo never understood this need to take on the weight of the world and its flurry of mismatches, or the mania for exploring blind alleys. There was no spirit of the transgressor in Inés, no tragic sense of liberation or revenge. Nor was she motivated by some kind of lust for knowledge. She was probably just a woman at odds with her era, a ship tossed by the rapids of history, at the tail end of the collapsing twentieth century. Though when you think about it, in what other century would Inés have fitted?

With sores raging in her mouth, wet shoes, and muddy socks, with her pleated skirt unironed for the first time (she would carefully fold it between sheets of paper each night, under the foam-rubber mattress), Inés turned up at seven in the evening at the Santisteban rope warehouse. Juan Rodríguez gestured from behind a tiny greasy window, and Inés leaned against a traffic light to wait for him, chilled to the bone.

Her teeth were chattering. Don Juan, who had been

scrutinizing her while he removed his overalls and put on his shiny jacket, didn't give her time to ask anything.

"You're coming with me," he murmured, in the tone of someone making an urgent, heroic decision. "You're in a fine state."

And Inés, moved, unable to open her mouth to express her boundless gratitude, obediently followed him.

Inés's disappearance didn't unduly concern Pumpi's friends. Ricardo and Elena were of the opinion that she'd gone off somewhere, and Carlota prophesied she wouldn't be back: "She left as she came."

Eduardo set about making inquiries and combed the city, tirelessly and without success. Time was pressing because he had decided to go off to Galicia for the September fiestas. He'd heard that the Galicians were big spenders in the fiestas and that they were fonder of music than the Moors. Eduardo woke up thinking what a good time Inés would have had there, what with the language being similar and all.

Don Juan Rodríguez didn't live on the outskirts of town, as his admirer had imagined—with those long, humiliating journeys to work on the metro crammed with contrite humanity—but quite near to where he worked, in Calle de las Huertas. It was a fifth-floor apartment with two bedrooms, a kitchen, bathroom, and living room with a balcony overlooking the street. Don Juan tended his goldfinches and ferns with great care.

"The geraniums," he said, "grow by themselves. You just have to pluck off the dry leaves."

Inés, enchanted with the plants and goldfinches, enjoyed with demure sweetness Don Juan's ministrations: the rubs, the aspirin with milk and brandy, lemon and bicarbonate gargles. The pneumonia was short-lived.

Anxious to repay him, she got him to come home every day for lunch. She prepared dishes more delicious than Don Juan could ever have dreamed of: partridge in leek sauce; raw grouper fillets with mint and grapefruit; chicory-flavored trout pie; roast veal stuffed with olives; Italian salads, fancy sponge cakes and chocolates. It was a diet accepted by Don Juan—a man of few words but very good manners—with some sighing and a great deal of dissimulation.

Inés, who showed no signs of wanting to leave and shamelessly abused his hospitality, struck him as a good but unhappy girl, a surprising young thing who could have been his daughter and whom he would have gladly adopted, had the circumstances been right.

He was, therefore, frankly surprised the first night she got into his bed. It wasn't, in fact, her getting into bed that surprised him—because he was fast asleep—but finding her there, naked and curled up in a ball beside him when he woke up in the morning.

For a moment Don Juan was afraid he'd committed some dreadful indiscretion. He calmed down, though, when he clearly remembered having gone to bed alone. He was on the point of waking her up and demanding an explanation—he was angry and had decided to tell her to leave immediately—but the expression on the girl's face stopped him. It was an expression of languid happiness, of a peacefulness yearned for, consummated, and fully embraced. A lock of hair lying across her cheek emphasized the delicate features of her face.

Don Juan got out of bed trying not to make a noise, showered, dressed, and, hardly stirring the air, ate breakfast in the cool of dawn. Only when he was about to leave did he remove the birds' cover so that they could burst into song. That was when he took a final glance around his bedroom. Inés had kicked off the sheet and appeared in all her splendid and unsuspecting nakedness. Don Juan held his breath. His first instinct was to cover her up. The stirrings of vertigo and the feeling he might collapse right there halted him, and he turned around and bolted down the stairs.

But the image of Inés naked, a shore of rosy delights, sensuality squandered in the sinuous braiding of her defenselessness, wouldn't leave him all day long. It seeped into his blood, was mistress of his conscience, pursued him between bills and delivery notes, playing hide and seek with the ledgers and forcing him to make more mistakes in a day than he'd made in his entire career.

Inés, who hadn't got a wink of sleep all night, pretending to sleep while he was getting up and intoxicated by her own temerity and the prize she'd won—his body smells, the smell of the mattress, an essence permeating the apartment, the sound of his innocent snoring, the feel of his chest, covered in gray hairs (old wolf, old bear)—finally fell into a pleasant swoon, a boat floating on the weightless drift of an Arcadian dream.

Just as she'd guessed, Don Juan didn't come home to eat. She waited for him between two and three to make sure and then went back to sleep. At seven, after ironing all the clothes and cleaning the whole apartment, she went out. She didn't want Don Juan to find her there or wanted at least to come back to knock on his door and give him the chance to reject her or accept her in her new role of lover.

It was already night and the new moon shone upon the humming jealous city when Don Juan realized it was her from the sound of the bell's ring, neither timid nor imperious.

He opened the door and lowered his eyes. Inés came in. Don Juan was listening to a basketball match on the radio. They both listened for a few minutes, until Inés switched the radio off. He kept still and said nothing. Inés did likewise. Later, she let it happen, as the goldfinches pecked at the bars.

Trembling and eager, Juan's hands had explored her entire body in search of the dream engendered that very morning by the beauty of the resplendent, sleeping form. Don Juan felt a dull ache in his heart as the moral incest was consummated, stretching his life's narrow and simple margins to breaking point.

Later on, a cold draft that cut through everything in its path had penetrated the cracks in the walls, and the two sinners had taken refuge in one another's arms and hearts, as though in the hot clasp of the earth, and had exorcised the north wind with a chaste, electric kiss that fused them without mediation in the compact darkness of sleep.

In the morning Inés discovered a new sensation in her body, the sum of memory struggling against the limbo of virginity, the vertigo of the causative rising and taking possession of her soul, transmitting to it taste, smell, touch, sight, and temperature.

She had felt very happy. For the first time her dark thirst for uncertainty—a strange thirst, always observed with wonder by Eduardo—was quenched: now more than ever nothing was clear, everything was confused, and now more than ever she knew peace, tasted the happiness distilled by each of the day's demands. She swept, cleaned, washed, gave lettuce to the goldfinches, even worried about the future of humanity she heard threatened on the radio by nuclear missiles, and every act fell into place, lodged itself fully in the narcotic coherence of her dream, in that wholeness only the gratuitous can supply.

That day, as a reward, she served Juan noodle soup and beefsteak with fried potatoes and canned tomatoes.

But that's when things started to go wrong. Juan didn't eat a bite and, contrary to habit, drank two glasses of wine, one after the other.

In the evening he came back a little drunk, and Inés struggled inwardly between anxiety and tenderness. In the end she decided to follow his lead, so both spent hours without saying a word. This didn't really bother her, though: it was just very nice to be there together.

"Maruja will be back in three days," he told her, late that night, when the only sounds they heard were the distant murmur of traffic on Paseo del Prado and the ticking of the wall clock.

Inés continued listening to the silence.

"You must leave tomorrow. I would have helped you like a daughter. But now . . ."

Inés smiled to herself, got up and went over to her good, awkward man, so as to silence him with a kiss.

"Inés, little Inés, you've read too many books!"

Inés turned around and shook her head.

"How could I, silly, when I can't read!"

Juan felt bad because she was clearly taking no notice of him. Annoyed, he shook off her arms, sat on the edge of the bed and switched the lamp on. In this light he was struck even more by the disparity between his gray-haired body with its rolls of fat and that of the trembling girl, as she looked at him with misty unseeing eyes.

"You're to leave tomorrow."

"Let's both go tomorrow," she suggested.

And that night, clothed in impeccable English tweed, Juan rode on horseback through beeches and oaks, climbed shapely hillocks that opened onto vast valleys from whose brilliance emerged shrill ducks flying in formation, describing the name of Inés, mistress and lady of his dreams. In the middle of the enormous forest, beyond the lakes, lay the ashen and surreal palace, encircled by fountains and ornamental gardens where peacocks and Indian pheasants dragged their tails.

Inside the palace, pale servants bowed as he passed. Flagstones echoed intimate ecstasies, and mirrors reflected metallic visitations, fleeting smiles that barely met. Chamber followed chamber, and the trills of a thousand caged birds gave wing to Don Juan's momentum. Finally, by the oval light of the skylight, with one hand offering sugar to a full-blooded Negro, and the other raising in welcome a glass of wine as red as her nipples, Inés awaited him, naked and milky white.

The following morning, with the goldfinch made a little tetchy by the knife sharpener's whistle and in a hurry because he was late, Don Juan stoically dismissed the matter. He didn't care whether Inés was really a fabulously rich heiress, recently come of age, or whether she wasn't.

He didn't care about palaces and groves, the life of luxury and the promise of eternal love. Nor did he care about the passion her ripe lips had implanted even in his entrails or the compassion her innocence inspired in him.

What he did care about—and this he saw clearly as he was shaving, sleep still in his eyes—was the respect he owed his wife.

True, he shared few pleasures with Maruja: a cheeky son, the unbeatable partnership they made at whist evenings, and little else. But loved or not, sick or well, ugly or pretty, she was truly his wife. Inés had squandered her secret in the belief that it could buy her what she most desired, or thought she desired, and believed herself therefore safe from pain. Juan didn't want to get involved in explanations and merely offered her a sweet.

"Look, Inés, you're just a child. You'd end up hating me. You'll thank me for this one day."

These words stung Inés, and she started to cry inconsolably.

Juan attempted to calm her down by treating her firmly. He sat on the bed and ordered her: "You've got to leave today, and don't come back around here again. Do you understand? For my sake!"

Inés offered solutions: he could bring Maruja, and Juan, and the goldfinches. There was room for all of them, and she'd give them work. They wouldn't even be lovers, if that's what respect for his wife demanded. Her voice was getting weaker and weaker, and as her sobbing stopped, almost without her noticing, the very feeling in her words dissolved in the solitude of the bedroom: Don Juan had left.

To love, to have loved, freely and without compromise.

Her entire horizon had been within those four walls. Now they had no place for her! They expelled her into the world without guide or reference point, to the desolate, inert span of life, houses and things, animals, machines, and people who could no longer rekindle any love and therefore lay down or moved on, bereft of all feeling, like Inés herself coming out of Calle de las Huertas like a sleepwalker, with no anger, or pain, or any thought, as though amputated from herself.

Her intention was probably to return to Calle Preciados.

Ricardo and Elena were no longer in Calle Preciados, which Don Juan carefully avoided on his route that day. All the Pumpi gang had gone off to Galicia, that promised land where it's always fiesta time.

Eduardo, struck by a thunderbolt of intuition, was nevertheless waiting for her. He knew that one way or another she would end up needing him, if only so she could, in that warm and aromatic voice, pour into his ear the vibrant compulsion of her final secret.

Eduardo let the hours torture him. Inés must be on her way. Inés was on her way.

But Inés, who had left Calle de las Huertas without any intent whatsoever, though maybe unconsciously heading for Preciados, never showed up there. Not that day, nor the next, nor any other. In the city of Madrid, in the twentieth century at least, no more was ever heard of Inés Pereira. She is now, forever, a question without reply.

Translated by John McCarthy

John Turner

Andrés Barba

SHE REALIZED WHAT WAS GOING ON when she
went downstairs and the wind banged open the front door
before she'd even touched it. It seemed like there was no
one there, but it was just that she couldn't see anyone. She
walked toward the Plaza Mayor as though floating on air,
and even the buildings seemed they'd move if you just
nudged them with your hand. She sat down. She thinks
she sat down lost in thought, because the first time she
heard the voice, she thought it was a boy, or a whistle, so

ANDRÉS BARBA *(Madrid, 1975–) has taught at Bowdoin
College in Maine and Universidad Complutense in Madrid. His first
novel,* El hueso que más duele, *was published in 1997. "John
Turner" is an excerpt from his second novel,* La hermana de Katia
*(2001). It is the story of a fourteen-year-old girl, Katia's sister, who
is never named. Though told in the third-person, the narrative is
intensely personal and gives an insight into the life of a less-than-
typical Madrid family. Mamá is a prostitute, Katia is a striptease
dancer, and "she," the sister, spends her time cooking and cleaning,
watching animal documentaries on television, and observing tourists
in Madrid's Plaza Mayor.*

she paid no attention, but then it touched her shoulder and she turned around because it was behind her, the hand that had touched her was behind her saying: "Hey, girl." Saying, "Hey, girl, are you all right." Saying it without asking it like a question, the way Katia does. "Are you all right, little girl."

She was going to say no, that when she left home she was not all right, that she had felt strange, like she was floating, and she remembered that she'd left everything unmade: the beds, lunch, everything; it was three days since she'd swept and had only just remembered, not quite sure why, just as she turned around and got nervous, all at once—it had never shaken her so badly before.

"Y . . . y . . . yes," she said thinking, now I won't be able to talk; now he'll ask me something else and I won't be able to say anything. He was wearing a white shirt. He was very handsome and suddenly she felt ugly, uglier than ever.

"Are you sure you're all right?"

And her: "Y . . . y . . . yes."

JESUS LOVES YOU, that was what his little black button said.

"What's your name?"

She answered, stuttering a little less but feeling uglier and uglier; if she turned one way she'd show her good side, but when he had called her she had turned the wrong way, neither pretty as a pin nor ugly as sin, that was what Mamá always said about her. She was about to run off, but for a minute she felt inexplicably comfortable and asked him what his name was.

"John. John Turner."

"John Turner," she repeated. "What does that mean?"

"It doesn't mean anything; it's just a name."

"Is it your father's name, too?"

"No, my father's name is Ernest," John said.

It seemed like the silence was going to be uncomfortable, but it wasn't.

"Do you know Jesus?"

"Jesus, the one on the cross?"

"Yes, do you know him?"

"Yes."

It was true; she did know him. Once she'd gone into a church and seen him hanging on his cross, covered in blood, pierced through the heart, his eyes staring up at heaven, begging for mercy, or forgiveness, or whatever, poor thing—that's what she thought about Jesus—poor thing hanging on that cross, dying, what had he done to deserve that? Pity, that's what she felt for lonely Jesus up there on his cross, and she didn't understand why that woman was kneeling down in front of him. Crying out of pity, maybe that was it, crying out of pity because nobody deserved to be treated like that. What had he done wrong? Had he wanted lots of blowjobs? But that wasn't wrong, that was what Mamá did and it wasn't wrong. Had he killed some-body? Stolen? Lied?

"What did they do that for?"

"What?" said John. "Nail him to the cross?"

"Yes."

"For being God," he replied, firing off the answer so fast it seemed learned by heart.

Jesus was God and that's why they'd nailed him up on a cross? Now, that really was totally incomprehensible.

"But was he good?"

Why did John laugh at her question? Was it stupid? And if it was stupid, then why had they nailed him up there on the cross? Wasn't that even more stupid?

"I don't understand."

"What don't you understand? Why they nailed him to the cross?"

"Yes."

"Men were evil, are evil, and will be evil, that's why they nailed him to the cross."

"Men aren't evil, they just want to get laid."

"Excuse me?"

John opened his eyes wide in surprise. She hadn't really thought about it, it was just one of those things Mamá said when she was on the phone, "Men aren't evil, they just want to get laid." Or, "Soon they won't even want me to give blowjobs," and though she didn't really know exactly what the words meant, she took them to be truisms.

"Excuse me, what did you say?"

"Well, you know," she said, a little embarrassed, ". . . *that*."

And she remembered that, in her haste to leave the house, she hadn't made the beds, she still had to make lunch, had to sweep the floor, and she said: "I have to go."

"Why?"

"I have chores to do."

John looked slightly annoyed and then said: "Listen, I am going to be in the plaza every afternoon next week. Why don't you come again another day?"

"What for?"

"We can talk about Jesus, if you want."

"Does it have to be about Jesus?"

She didn't want to talk about Jesus, every time John mentioned him she thought of him up there on his lonely cross. They'd killed him and he hadn't even been bad, she thought, they killed him just for being God. There were plenty of other things they could talk about, they could go to a café and he could say to her, "Order whatever you want, don't worry about the prices, for once in your life don't worry about how much anything costs," and she'd say, "Tomato juice." She'd always loved tomato juice, and then she'd ask him where he was born, what the people were like there, if there were rivers, or seas, or mountains nearby, if they talked a lot or were silent, if they spoke English or French or German, and she'd ask him to say a few words just to hear what it sounded like. "So, how do you say 'I'd like a tomato juice, please,' in your language?" and she'd learn a thousand other things from John Turner if he didn't talk to her about Jesus, not that she had anything against him, just because he made her feel pity. Would he understand that? Would he understand that Jesus filled her with pity? It was nice being with John, his blue eyes, crew cut, big nose and, beneath it, those thin lips straight out of a watercolor painting; that was why she wanted to know if it had to be Jesus that they talked about, because she really didn't want to end up getting sad again if she met up with him another day.

"We can talk about whatever you want," said John Turner.

"Thank you," she said without looking at him, getting slightly embarrassed again but without knowing why this time, maybe because he'd said they didn't have to talk about Jesus.

When she got home and heard Mamá screaming, her happiness came crashing down. Jorge had come to lunch. Sometimes Jorge came over; he was Mamá's boyfriend. He worked in a butcher's shop, and he was the one who had gotten Katia her job at the produce market. After what happened that morning, he had come over to tell Mamá about it. They fought. Katia had locked herself in the bathroom and Mamá was yelling at her to come out right this minute, to not make her any madder than she already was. Katia came out in silence, her face all mad. Mamá asked what the fuck she thought she was doing, throwing a melon at the lady who owned the market, what she thought they were supposed to do now, and Katia told her about the job at the stripclub. Mamá didn't like it one bit. Mamá went all serious.

"It doesn't have to come to that," she said. "You're still young, you're only . . ."

"Eighteen," Katia said, indignant that Mamá didn't know how old she was.

"Eighteen," Mamá repeated. "Jorge, say something to this child."

"What do you want me to say? She's eighteen . . ."

For a minute everybody was quiet. It was probably just a second, but it seemed like a long time.

"I'm leaving, I have to get back to work," said Jorge, but no one paid any attention to him. He left slowly, like he was trying not to bother anybody, and the three of them stood there in the hallway not looking at each other; Katia in the

bathroom door, Mamá opposite Katia, and she at the front
door, Mamá not looking mad anymore, just unhappy, Katia
not looking indignant at not having her age remembered
anymore but with the vague apology on her lips, the apology of someone who knows she has disappointed someone,
and as for herself . . . she wasn't even there; only Katia and
Mamá, Katia not knowing what to do, playing with the
handle on the bathroom door, Mamá. . . . How long had
Mamá been wearing that expression? Mamá, who was
never sad, looked sad right then.

"Daughter," she said, she who never said "daughter" and
only ever said "Katia" said, "Daughter."

And Katia must have realized because she looked up
right away. She looked like she was going to say "Mamá,"
but she didn't say "Mamá" she said: "What?" Maybe she
wanted to say "Mamá," but she said, "What?"

And Mama said, "Be careful."

And Katia, "OK."

And so she wouldn't have to stay any longer she put an
end to the conversation. "Well, I have to go. Jorge is waiting for me."

And as she walked to the door she put her hand on
Katia's shoulder and let it slide down to her elbow, not
exactly being affectionate—Mamá wasn't affectionate—
and then she closed the door and Katia said, "I got the job."
She remembered everything. The way she had left home
that afternoon, the Plaza Mayor, the tourists, and of
course his blue eyes and the JESUS LOVES YOU button.
She, who forgot everything so easily, surprised herself
remembering John's words, she repeated them exactly as
she would have if she had just heard them, and she re-

membered the way he moved his hands, the way he smiled, and listened in silence. She had written his name all over a piece of paper, covered it completely, changing styles, sometimes normal and sometimes imagining his signature, *John Turner,* JOHN TURNER, john turner, it sounded like a famous person's name, it had a ring to it, sounded like it should be in headlines, "the well-known singer John Turner . . ." no, not a singer, "the famous biologist John Turner returning from his African expedition," yes, much better, a biologist, "has just published his study on the animals of the Serenghetti . . ." getting out of a car or off of a boat in his safari suit, his mud-caked boots, and, yes, his JESUS LOVES YOU button, why not.

She had only gone to look for him once. She looked in the plaza and then in the surrounding streets and then walked back to the viaduct. She thought that if she came back later maybe she'd have more luck; maybe John had gotten hungry, or had to go to the bathroom and had just left. She went back to the plaza and that's where it struck her: maybe if she looked in a church she'd find him. It had become dark ridiculously fast that afternoon when she saw it in the corner, almost hidden behind one of the plaza's arches. The stone at the entrance was rugged to the touch. When she opened the door it smelled like must and lilies. A man dressed in white stood behind the altar with his arms open wide, in a cross, and the people were saying, "I believe in one God, the Father Almighty, Creator of all things, visible and invisible."

She was scared. She considered going up to the front to look for John but the rapture of that voice, speaking in unison and in monotone, paralyzed her.

"And in one Lord Jesus Christ, the only-begotten Son of God, begotten of the Father before all worlds, God of God, Light of Light, True God from True God, begotten, not made." What were they all doing standing there, what was going to happen now, why was that man looking at her like she was doing something wrong? "who, for us men, and for our salvation, came down from heaven," why didn't they leave, why didn't they sit down, yes, they should sit down, and that man in white behind the altar should lower his arms and stop staring at her, scared, he was making her scared, "and was incarnate by the Holy Spirit of the Virgin Mary, and was made man, and was crucified also for us under Pontius Pilate. He suffered and was buried," talking about Jesus again, with him right there, all alone, as always, up there on his little cross by the altar, looking straight ahead and upward, this one wasn't as bloody but he had that same sad, impassive expression, "and the third day he rose again according to the Scriptures, and ascended into heaven, and sitteth on the right hand of the Father. And he shall come again with glory to judge both the quick and the dead, whose kingdom shall have no end," and she thought John must not be there, he must not be standing up there, all serious, his voice blending in with everyone else's, sounding like just one voice and one person; she thought she'd like to run to Katia, even though that was impossible, it was late and she would be practicing her striptease number by now, up-down, up-down, up-down, one-two, one-two, one-two, "I believe in the Holy Spirit, the Lord and Giver of Life, who proceedeth from the Father and the Son, who with the Father and the Son together is worshiped and glorified," one-two, one-two—because you had to count in your head

Black Oaks

Dulce Chacón

GOING BACK TO BLACK OAKS was not easy for any of the maids who had enlisted in the militia. Some returned with scarves wrapped low on their foreheads in an effort to hide the humiliation of their shaved heads. But Isidora came back with her long locks intact, cascading in disorderly fashion onto her shoulders. Unlike the other women, Isidora would not have to raise her eyes little by little as her hair began to grow. However, when she found herself forced to receive the Marqués and Marquesa de Senara with Quica's daughter, she could not face the par-

DULCE CHACÓN (Zafra, Badajoz, 1954–) is a poet, playwright, and novelist whose writing often gives women a voice in situations such as war and domestic abuse where they tend to go unheard. The selection included here was taken from her novel Cielos de barro, for which she won the Azorín Prize in 2000. "Black Oaks" describes the servant Isidora's return to the ranch where she lives and works in Extremadura. Having left to join a Republican militia during the civil war, she was raped by Fascists before returning, defeated. Isidora hides her secret from her husband and from Quica, an orphan who has arrived to work on the ranch and does not know that her own mother was also raped before being murdered.

ents of the two men who had witnessed her disgrace. Her eyelids veiled the fear in her eyes as she lowered her gaze; she thought she would never lift it again. For Isidora, returning to the ranch meant believing that she would remain eternally humiliated.

Doña Carmen arranged everything so that her servant Isidora would keep the secret that had to be kept. She assured Isidora, in front of her boyfriend Modesto, that she would never turn her in for having been in the militia or for having killed the soldier who murdered Quica; she brought forth the dead woman's medallion and mentioned Isidora's confession in front of her daughter Victoria as evidence. Doña Carmen said nothing about Isidora's rape. And left nothing out of her plan. As soon as she was finished telling Modesto about the danger Isidora was in, she told him he could go back to the kitchen with Justa. Once alone with the servant, before ordering her to go and receive Quica's daughter, Doña Carmen asked her if she had had relations with her boyfriend.

"You mean, if I'm related to him?"

"If you've slept with him, Isidora."

"And why do I have to tell you?"

"In case you're pregnant. If you've been with him, the child could be his."

Isidora told her that she'd been with Modesto for the first and only time before she left for the front. So Doña Carmen provided Modesto with a piece of arable land and ordered him to build a house there so that he and Isidora could be married immediately.

And they were married, in the sacristy of the parish church, where, to satisfy the demands of Father Matías, both had previously sworn to renounce their socialist ideals. The priest had refused to officiate the sacrament of marriage unless both the bride and groom recanted their convictions. The groom swore in order to save the bride's life without knowing that she swore the same to save his. Doña Carmen signed as the witness.

The couple moved into the house that Modesto built in less than a month on the outer grounds of the farm. The newlywed wife rushed to and from Black Oaks, always on the run, fearful of meeting those she never wanted to see again. She knew that inevitably they would meet, that the Marqués de Senara's sons would cross her path. She ran. And every morning before she ran, after her husband had gone out to the fields, she would climb up onto the nightstand, jump heavily to the floor, and then maneuver a parsley stalk up inside herself to undo what she was afraid destiny had done. After repeated jumps from the nightstand, she ran until exhausted, feeling she had a deep wound that only her bleeding could heal.

But Isidora could have saved herself the trouble because her womb was not pregnant, there was no cause for embarrassment. She discovered this one afternoon upon getting up from a cattail chair where she had been sewing. Joaquina was beside her redoing the hem on a blue dress. She told Isidora that she had stained her skirt and was surprised when she saw her smile.

"Girl, you got no heart or spine? Hasn't anyone told you that having children makes a happy marriage?"

"If they're children sent by God, Joaquina."

"Well, damn! Who else would send them? Don't you want to get pregnant?"

"Now I do."

"Whoever gets what you're up to can have you, hon. Me, I'd give my life for Marciano to have given me a child before he died. Or two."

Finally, her wound was bleeding. She ran home backward to wash and change and to return clean. Clean. She wrung out her skirt, beating it against the wood with all her strength and fury. Upon returning to the farm, she gave in to the need she had denied herself until that point: to hug Quica's daughter.

Since the little one had come to the farm, Isidora had made it a point not to pay much attention to her. When the lady of the house told her to introduce the little girl to housework and then warned her that the child did not know and should never find out that her mother had been raped before she died, Isidora brought her to the back patio without looking at her. She did not want the child to see the memories rushing over Isidora's face whenever she looked at her. And she did not want to see the blade she'd ripped out of the murderer's hand reflected in the scar on the girl's face. She refused to remember that man's too-wide eyes as he lay panting and moaning over Quica's slit throat, too absorbed with his booty to notice her arrival, too absorbed to notice that his hand had relaxed and let go of his dagger. She did not want to see another look on the face of the washwoman's child, the look of degradation in Quica's eyes that Isidora herself had closed after picking up the medallion her friend had held very close to her lips.

The child said that she wasn't feeling well as soon as she set foot out of the car. She vomited everything in her stomach even before Isidora could prepare her a chamomile tea.

It was Justa who had held her forehead in one hand while with the other, she soaked the back of her neck with cold water.

"Girl, never once in my life have I seen someone spew like that. You're not doin' too well, are you. You're more yellow than a watermelon in winter."

"I'm fine, it's just that piece of junk—it jiggles me around like a badly saddled mule."

When the girl was feeling better, Isidora asked her what she knew how to do. She answered that she was a washgirl just like her mother. The next morning, Isidora put a small basin and washboard in the kitchen. She started by giving her small garments, things she thought she could manage, but the little one's skill and speed proved that she could take charge of the entire load right away. The child washed during the mornings, while Isidora tended to the Albuera's ill daughter. And while Isidora sewed during the afternoons, the little girl tended to the novice nun. That was the way Isidora wanted it—so she wouldn't see her. So that the little girl wouldn't discover her mother's raped face in her own. So that she would never be able to guess.

But that afternoon, when she found out that God hadn't made her with child, Isidora wanted to hug Quica's daughter, the little girl God had put in her life whom she had not wanted to accept. She hoped to give her the affection she had held back since the day the orphan girl arrived at Black Oaks, with half her face in bandages.

Translated by Barbara D. Riess

Sentimental Journey

Juan Goytisolo

IMPERCEPTIBLY, THE SIGNS ACCUMULATE. Scattered insidiously, treacherously, at irregular intervals, as if spaced out deliberately to make it difficult for you to read them. Not just the physical deterioration you hardly notice in daily life, the greater efforts required in all the routines and petty rituals, not even the anger and surprise, the instinctive rebellion—quickly suppressed—when you are suddenly confronted with a faded photograph from your youth: rather the brutal blow that strikes, at a carefree, happy moment, smashing through plans and calculations, and delivers you without defenses to awareness of inevitable decrepitude.

JUAN GOYTISOLO *(Barcelona, 1931–) went to Paris in "voluntary" exile in 1956 and has never returned to live in Spain. He now lives in Marrakesh. His prose and essays distinguish him as the contemporary Spanish writer who has made the strongest impact on the international world of writing and the younger generation of Spanish writers. This extract is from the first volume of his autobiography,* Forbidden Territory, *in which he describes his childhood and life as an angry young man of letters from the perspective of a writer gently but profoundly wielding the scalpel of poetic self-analysis.*

You are driving, for instance, at daybreak through a quiet, luminous countryside, along a peaceful, almost deserted side road and have forgotten, in fact, as you later discover, that it is Friday the thirteenth and that you are also in French département thirteen: all of which anyone remotely superstitious could interpret, albeit mistakenly, as an act of provocation. You brake at the stop sign by the junction with the main Saint Rémy-Tarascon road in response to a call from a middle-aged individual carrying a battered old suitcase on the other side of the crossroads: he wants a lift to a nearby town and once you realize it's on your route, you cross the road, after a brief exchange of words, forgetting even to look left, and suddenly hear a violent screech of brakes, seconds before the crash reduces your car to a sad heap of scrap metal. You stagger out of your car, confront the truck driver's waxen face, contorted by fear, an innocent bearer of a warning from destiny and Arab into the bargain. You say a few soothing words to him in his own language and then listen as he stammers out—not at all surprised by the fact that this seemingly injured European speaks his language—a half-whispered recitation of the *Kulchi fi yid Allah* and other respectful formulas from the Scriptures interwoven with exclamations of thanksgiving. An unlikely dialogue on the glass-strewn road. You don't yet feel any pain from the thumbnail that is hanging off, as you notice the indirect cause of the accident running off at top speed, suitcase on shoulder, and the shopkeeper at the crossroads lets you telephone the friend with whom you were staying and then pockets the price of the call without a murmur. Only confusion at your presence in this hazy, ghostly world, an object of the pity or idle chatter of the inevitable spectators, next to the aged, skinny figure of the helpless Moorish fruit-transporter who, after the shock, is also striving to establish the simple facts of the case—what damage, whose responsibility, the need to inform his boss, while you await the arrival of the police.

Or fifteen months later in the course of a sentimental journey to a region you have written about, after visiting the lonely, rural landscape, the setting for the plot of one of your novels, returning to the spot as the guilty man always revisits the scene of his crime, engulfed by a noisy, high-spirited throng of fans who have come from every corner of the province to witness, like you, the cruel, expiatory ceremony of the penning of the bulls. You perch on the wooden barrier in the lower square in Elche de la Sierra, through which the beasts will soon pound with their retinue of oxen and farmhands to a chorus of shouts and exploding fireworks, running away, attacking, climbing, delighting, and exciting the motley crowd; you move away from the human swarm, walk on up the street with your friends behind the rear guard, toward the parish church, trying to predict from the screams and hastily beaten retreats when the horns will come back from the square, the fenced-off square where the bulls will be fought and executed hours afterward in the bloody, collective ritual: after a long wait, you go down a side street that has been barricaded off, deaf to the warnings of your friend from Albacete who knows the lay of the land better than you—the length of the walk to the church, the lack of refuge points and barriers over which to climb in case of dire necessity—intent on reaching the stockade where the bulls are kept: you get to the opening onto the square and from the gap in the upright, wooden palisade, assess the difficulty of clambering in without drawing the attention of one of the animals, which already excited by the exploding firecrackers and the noise of sticks and clubs is pawing the ground, gazing stubbornly at the exit, anxious to attack, break through, and take revenge on the wily gang of boys who mock and mistreat it; you look for a safe place on your left as the beast lowers its head, charges quickly at the opening in the fence, and thunders past the farmhands, you hear the cries of terror when it catches one of them in full flight, throws him on the floor, gouges the body with its horns, and then abandons him for dead, facedown, and continues its outraged chase; again you hear the uproar announcing the second bull and notice your neighbors sneak away and climb up the barricades on the right, hauled up by the people above them, for a second time, you cling rashly to the left corner, trapped between a wall and the vertical logs of the barricade; suddenly realize that the bull has crossed the opening and instead of moving forward to attack those speeding off into the distance, it has turned round and is squaring up to you, barely two meters away, it stares at you for endless moments, just time for you to consider calmly, in pure amazement, the unthinkable situation you are in: your back to the corner, no way of getting over the barricades, aware of the absurdity of the scene, in suspense, your mind in a thick fog of disbelief; you try slowly to move toward the gate, convinced it is impossible this is really happening to you, that you are the protagonist in some sort of daydream, the usual, nightly, opaque, exhausting, persistent nightmare; yet you feel the blow from its head that knocks you down, drags you on your face across the ground, all notions of time and place disappear, seconds, unimaginable seconds, no panic, no pain, no anxiety, only, only, only an overwhelming sense of unreality; you then hear a friendly cry, your name howled rather than shouted out, moments before anonymous hands pull you up

by your arms, sit you up, rescue you; as you look up, you can
see Abdelhadi between the horns of the bull, hoisted up like
an empty carton by the furious beast, about to be flung backward by a toss of its head until, whipped by youths after a
brief, spectacular fall to the ground, the animal gets up, for-
gets your savior, half turns and races, enraged, after the gang.
There is movement, concern, belated, untimely offers of
help from those huddled around you and Abdelhadi; you are
almost flown through the air to the nearby first-aid post,
both wanting with the wounded pride of someone who has
just tripped in public to stop people from taking pity, to be
removed as quickly as possible from their curious gaze; you
grasp at once, far from the surrounding bustle, the grotesque,
comic twist of fortune that has hit you on exactly the same
day as a wretched spur-of-the-moment torero died impaled
on a bull's horns in the ring at Albacete in front of millions
of future televiewers; you are determined to hide this humiliation from Monique, especially from her, before it is con-
sumed, digested, exorcised, days, weeks, months, or years
later, thanks to that slow, gradual, internal process leading
secretly to the act of writing; you are identified, treated, your
bumps and bruises disinfected with Mercurochrome and
cotton and like sleepwalkers acknowledge the admiring
homage of a corporal in the Civil Guard, witness to the
accident, who slaps Abdelhadi on the shoulder several times,
tries in vain to communicate with him, and then turns to you
and clumsily formulates his compliment: your friend,
though an Arab, is noble and brave.

Just like a frustrated mother after an unwelcome miscar-
riage wishes to overcome her trauma and impatiently
searches for a suitable opportunity to become pregnant

again, you suddenly feel in the bedroom where you are recovering from the blow the violent urge to write rise up after months of sterility, the urgency and need to write, express yourself, not to allow all that you love, your past experience, emotions, what you are and have been, to disappear with you, determination to fight tooth and claw against oblivion, that black abyss with open jaws that lies in wait, you well know, around any corner, to capture the precious gift of life, the human miracle, the reluctant concessions of existence and reality, you delight in your five senses' confirmation that the daily portent is being extended, that a chance postponement allows you to be yourself, sudden, repeated floods of memories, flashes in the pan, snapshots, will-o'-the-wisps, an intoxication with seeing, touching, smelling, stroking, evoking the past, History, histories, the linking of facts, imponderables, circumstances that have changed you into this misused body stretched out on your back on the bed in the narrow room where you are staying, a moment relived now almost two years later at the touch of a pen when you begin to order your impressions and feelings, shape them on the blank page, abridged reminiscences, like waves breaking, subject to your wandering memory, imperative to tell others and yourself what you were and are not, whom you might have been and have not become, to clarify, correct, complete the reality elaborated in your successive fictions, the single book, the Book you have been creating and recreating for twenty years and as you invariably note, at the end of each of its chapters, that you still have not written.

Translated by Peter Bush

Right All Along
Fernando Quiñones

THEY LOOKED AT EACH OTHER and, deep in their eyes, there was a faint question mark right next to the huge exclamation mark of their victory. But does he know? each one wondered. Yes, he had to know. Had they been British, they would have flashed the V sign as a friendly greeting. It was, after all, a quality victory written up in the newspapers and gloriously broadcast over the radio. Luciano's nose was, indeed, red enough to clearly indicate that, since his youth, he had dutifully served under the wine flag whose absolute triumph had just been announced to the world. Fair-skinned Antón, on the other hand, seemed as unlike a drunk as can be imagined.

FERNANDO QUIÑONES *(1930–98) was a much-loved native of Cádiz. A prize-winning poet, novelist, journalist, essayist, and short story writer, his writing is firmly rooted in Andalusia. He is known for his love of the local language, land, and sea. After his death, the Fernando Quiñones Foundation was established to award an annual prize for literature. The story "Right All Along" comes from his collection* Cinco historias del vino *(1960) and presents two old-time Seville characters with one foot in the modern world and the other in tradition.*

But let's clarify: upon reading this word, *drunk*, only certain small minds would consider it dishonorable. We believe, along with all spirited spirits, that a drunk is often certainly someone very sad, and, in the worst sense of the word, is in the grip of a condition that should not exist for others to see. But it is also apparent that a drunk, even when thoroughly drunk, can stay within the boundaries of behavior considered acceptable by the most straitlaced of people provided that the latter retain a spark of imagination and of kindness. We are, then, in the company of two dear old drunks of the best kind, who practice the habit without ever allowing it to destroy them. Antón and Luciano, in short, are drunks even though they are not British; even though their fingers did not flash the victory V in greeting; and even though they do not find themselves either in a dive near Picadilly or at a Southampton party such as the one I attended where the most dignified of local dignitaries reached the loftiest heights of that splendid state when they did not entirely lose their dignity upon falling off their chairs at the end of the evening. Antón and Luciano are Spanish subjects, born and bred in the populous city of Seville, which in no way implies that they are just vegetating their way toward retirement like characters in an Andalusian farce.

Times have changed and now life in Seville can be rushed, with first-rate business opportunities, air travel, industrial activity, and a fervor for gambling that's apt to burn in the bosoms of its most sheltered ladies and shatter the restful seclusion of inner courtyards with gently gurgling fountains. The area around Triana, all bell towers and gypsy melodies, its streets once teeming with bulls and song, is now labeled something like Plan 4, Zone F. On the shore of the Guadalquivir River where Motamid—Moorish king and poet—cried real tears, there is a section known as the Silver Meadows, more bountiful in verses and benedictions than in actual water. It will be the site of a group of prefabricated dwellings that are sure to bring their builders plenty of publicity, if not necessarily respect for their love of beauty. Some parts of downtown Seville can, at times, look painfully similar to parts of downtown Berlin, or Madrid, or Houston. In its taverns Coke competes with the exceptional wines from Jerez, their own *finos* and *amontillados*. Any silly stunt of its soccer team provokes more barbershop talk than the latest fresh-faced aspiring bullfighter recently emerged from San Bernardo or La Macarena, the poorer sections of town. In short, Seville is suffering from acute cerebral spasms due to one of the most dramatic situations in which an illustrious and soulful city can find itself: the battle against overpopulation and, particularly, against new lifestyles. In places like Italy and France, for example, they have, up to now, been able to deal with this situation with exquisite taste and common sense. Fortunately, there are still old-fashioned people and traditional customs to be found in Seville. There are still courtyards where the wind whispers among lemon and lime trees, places and faces that keep alive the most secret and refined aspects of the city that once was. Urban Seville, thank God, has still not entirely supplanted graceful Seville, and its hundreds of thousands of citizens have not yet, and forever, snuffed out the music and the majesty of horse-drawn carriages and the Giralda Tower. Luckily as well, the likes of Mr. Papowtwegoo, Mrs. Hiltontrent, or Mr. Florinoff, makers of plastic souvenirs and miniature Virgin keepsakes, have not altogether succeeded in overshadowing our own Ben Zumruk, Manuel Torres, Rafael Gómez, or Gustavo Bécquer.

So there they are, posed between sunshine and drizzle. Their lives and finances warmed by the sunshine of the new, yet their blood and their charm drizzled with the not-for-profit ways of old. With one foot in the new riverside developments and the other in Lorca's starry Guadalquivir, our two drinkers from Seville are an apt reflection of their times. They know nothing of the schemes, the tricks, or the reckless inclinations of those who exist hand-to-mouth; their income comes from trading cattle and the occasional sale of land or a millionaire's estate on the green valleys around Jerez. Only once, stretching to reach farther than legendary giant Briareo, did Luciano take part in the sale of a house in Cádiz, a house that jutted out into the ocean like an old galleon, its stucco cracked by the salty sunlight and, crowning its small tower like some diminutive port-dwelling king, a black cat scrutinizing the seas. In any case, our two friends make a perfectly decent living manipulating numbers, using their two eyes, and doing a lot of standing around in bars usually followed, after a quick call home, by lunch at Gayanos or Calvillo where the deals are really sealed. Seville, where they came into this world, gave them both their way of talking and their way of living, which is not necessarily stress-free nowadays, although life in the south can still feel and sound so very relaxed. Only a philosopher from New Zealand could fail to be fascinated by such a paradox. Furthermore, these two friends have never been rivals because they operate in different territories, the borders of which are scrupulously respected, and there are plenty of cattle, land, and bricks to go around. So today they meet and are content. They have won one of their longest and fiercest battles. Today they are not just light-headed consumers of Jerez wines, but rather two clear-sighted and sharply intuitive individuals. It's been all over the newspapers and the radio: wine, particularly wine from Jerez, protects against numerous diseases and cures a host of others. Up to now Luciano and Antón have cultivated their love of wine together, but always without much talk about it. Jerez wines have been witness—before disappearing inside them—to the spectacle of their talk-animated faces, but seldom to any mention of their virtues. Today, however, it's time to speak about them—once and for all—since it is no longer a vague feeling of guilt before a half-empty bottle of *amontillado*, of *solera* or *palo cortado* that unites them.

"Sooo . . . not many people here today, eh?"

As usual the bar is almost empty at noontime. But it's a pleasure to take the long way around to what one really wants to say.

"I ran into Zenón yesterday. At the club."

"And what'd he say about the Huelva deal?"

"You mean La Palma. It seems the owner backed out at the last minute."

"Pedrito, *two*."

They always say it just like that, *two*, with no further details. It's perfectly clear. The spry barman reaches for the *fino* bottle and the sherry sings its way into the glasses, lithe and graceful as Mozart's music, like Picasso's strokes of blue, red, green, like the budding breasts of early spring. The friends look at each other. And they get to the point.

"Did you read *ABC* today? . . . About wine . . ."

"I heard it on the radio."

"Good news, eh? Interesting." Antón probes.

"It's a real thrill." Luciano capitulates.

"Actually, it makes little difference to me," Antón backs off guardedly. "You know I can take it or leave it."

Luciano, serious and bordering on irritation, looks him in the eye.

"Same with me, but still."

Ever since he was a child Antón has been unable to bring himself to agree with any statement except little by little.

"Well," he edits, "it's always a thrill to hear about things that a person is allowed to do."

"But you won't count yourself among those who get upset by the findings, that's for sure," Luciano hammers.

"It's just that . . ."

"That nothing. We love wine. And now it turns out that it's not only not harmful, it's even good for you."

They are quiet, solemnly so. A ray of sunlight reaches through the door and lands squarely on the good-natured bar mascot, a dusty turtle lounging under the box of the shoeshine boy surrounded by cigarette butts and used matches. Outside a street vendor is hawking his wares.

"Two more," Luciano breaks the pause.

Antón's eyes follow the trajectory of the bottle's flight between the shelf and their glasses. There are six other customers at the counter, and small plates of *tapas* appear next to their full or empty glasses: the amber gleam of clams, silent and so perfectly lifeless; the dazzling plumpness of the hake fish; the green, red, and yellow chaos of the salad. But no little dishes—empty or full—are placed by Luciano's or

Antón's glasses. The barman, who's been serving them day in and day out, knows that they never eat with their wine. They do not care to have anything disturb the country-flavored lash of the dry *amontillado* on their throats. Or the *fino's* lengthy greeting to the palate. Or the soothing and nautical bull's-eye of the *manzanilla*. "One should never eat with Jerez," they claim. "Food just ruins it."

"So, the property in La Palma . . ."

"Forget it, the deal's off. Fill her up."

"And the one in Carmona . . ."

"That one might work out. All the way up!"

This time the barman's hands need not make a long trip. Why pretend? It's common knowledge that don Luciano and don Antón never have fewer than six rounds. So the bottle remains casually close to the glasses that are empty once again.

"Yes, it seems that we were right all along," Luciano declares.

"That's right," Antón finally concedes, in his own reserved if categorical way.

"I can tell you that wine certainly never upset my system. And, I do drink quite a lot, about as much as you, though I'm no drunk. I just can't see how it could hurt anyone."

A diminutive white radio miraculously thunders out the third movement of Tchaikovsky's *Pathétique.* A young boy stands at the door. He carries a wineskin and peeks inside before bolting away like lightning.

"Those idiots," Luciano mutters not without a touch of resentment.

"What idiots?"

"All those people who were always claiming that wine

causes this and that illness. Just look at this glass. How can it be bad for you? Look at it like this, against the sun."

Almost without moving the glass he empties it, in three slow, appreciative sips. The wine's bouquet hangs in the air for an instant. Suddenly, Antón and Luciano burst out laughing. They giggle long and softly, like two schoolboys who have gotten away with some mischief. And the wine continues singing in the glasses of those who did know, before anyone scientifically proved it, that life goes better with wine.

"Fill it."

Translated by Cristina de la Torre

Holy Week in Granada

Federico García Lorca

THE CAREFREE TRAVELER, all smiles and locomotive screeches, goes to the festival of Las Fallas in Valencia. The bacchanalian, to Holy Week in Seville. The one who burns with longing for bared bodies, to Malaga. The melancholy contemplative, to Granada, to be alone in the atmosphere imbued with basil, shadowy moss, and nightingale trills that flow from the old hills next to the blaze of saffron, the deep grays, and blotting-paper pink that are the walls of the Alhambra. To be alone. To contemplate an environment filled with dissonant voices and breathe an air so beautiful it is almost thought, at a nerve center of Spain where St. John of the Cross's Castilian poetry is suffused with cedar, cinnamon, and fountains and brings to Spanish mysticism that Eastern

FEDERICO GARCÍA LORCA *(Granada, 1898–1936) is the best known and most translated Spanish writer of the twentieth century. In 1931 he founded and directed the itinerant Republican theater group, La Barraca. He was executed by Fascists near Granada at the beginning of the civil war. This piece, although from his first book published in 1918, already reveals a Lorcan poetic style in its impressionistic descriptions of Spain.*

air, that wounded, love-sick stag watching from a hill-
top.

To be alone, with the solitude one seeks in Florence;
to understand how the play of water is not a game as in
Versailles, but water as passion, water as agony.

Or to be in loving company and see spring vibrate within
the trees, through the skin of the delicate marble columns,
while the yellow spheres of lemons climb the ravines, casting
aside the snow, which flees in fright. If you want to feel that
sweet ticktock of blood on your lips next to the bull's hot
breath, go to the baroque tumult of world-famous Seville; if
you want to join a gathering of ghosts and perhaps find a
magical old ring in the labyrinth of your heart, go inland, to
hidden Granada. Of course, the traveler will be pleasantly
surprised that in Granada there is no Holy Week. Holy Week
does not suit the Christian, antispectacular character of the
people of Granada. When I was a child, the procession of the
Holy Burial appeared a few times, but only a few times
because the wealthy of Granada didn't always want to pay for
this parade. Over the last few years, with strictly commercial
zeal, they have organized processions lacking the solemn
poetry of the Holy Week of my childhood. Back then, it was
a Holy Week of lace, of canaries flying between the candles
on floats, of a tepid, mournful mood, as if all day it had been
asleep on the opulent bosoms of stout Granadan spinsters
out for a stroll on Holy Thursday, yearning for some officer,
judge, or foreign professor to take them away. The whole city
was like a merry-go-round moving slowly in and out of strik-
ingly beautiful churches, a fantasy akin to tunnels of death
and theatrical apotheosis. There were altars sown with wheat,
altars with waterfalls, others simple and threadbare, like a

cherished fairground booth: one, entirely of reeds, like a heavenly henhouse made of fireworks, and another, immense, with the cruel purple and ermine of Calderón's sumptuous poetry.

In a house on Calle Colcha, the street where they sell coffins and funeral wreaths for the poor, those who were to be Roman *soldaos* met to rehearse. These soldiers were not a brotherhood, like the lively warriors who escort the wondrous Macarena. They were people for hire: porters, shoeshine boys, patients recently discharged from the hospital trying to make some quick cash. They wore red beards like Schopenhauer, agitated cats, or intense professors. The captain was skilled in the military mode and taught them to mark a rhythm that went, "porón . . . chas!" at which point they struck the ground with their lances, to deliciously comic effect. As an example of local Granadan wit, I'll tell you that one year the Roman soldiers couldn't get anything right in rehearsal and spent more than two weeks furiously pounding their lances without coming together. The desperate captain finally yelled, "Enough, enough! No more banging, because if we go on this way we'll end up carrying lances in candlesticks," a popular saying repeated now by several generations in Granada.

I would beg my fellow citizens to restore the old Holy Week, to hide out of good taste that horrifying station of the Last Supper, and not desecrate the Alhambra, which is not and never will be Christian, with cacophonous processions, where what passes for good taste is mere vulgarity and only serves as an excuse for the crowds to trample the laurel, crush the violets, and urinate by the hundreds on the illustrious walls of poetry.

Granada should preserve for itself and for the traveler its inner Holy Week, so inner and so still that I remember how the breeze from the valley came in to the Calle de Gracia, astonished, and went all the way to the fountain in Plaza Nueva without encountering noise or song.

Because that way its snowy springtime will be perfect, and the intelligent traveler, with the message that the festival conveys, can engage in conversation with classic characters. With Ganivet's man of the sea, whose eyes linger on the hidden lilies of the River Darro; with the observer of twilight, who climbs longingly to his rooftop terrace; with the lover of the shape of the Sierra, who never goes near the mountains; with the gorgeous, sultry beauty eager for love, who sits with her mother in the small gardens; with a whole town full of admiring, obliging people, surrounded by unique natural beauty, who expect nothing and can only smile.

Through an amazing variety of shapes, landscapes, light, and smells, the unsuspecting traveler will experience the sensation that Granada is the capital of a kingdom with its own art and literature, and will find a curious mixture of Jewish Granada and Moorish Granada apparently buried by Christianity yet still alive and incorruptible in its own unawareness.

The impressive mass of the cathedral, the great imperial Roman seal of Carlos V, does not blot out the small tent of the Jew who prays before an image made from the silver of a seven-armed candelabra, just as the tombs of the Catholic monarchs have not prevented the occasional appearance of the crescent moon on the breast of Granada's finest sons. The struggle continues hidden and unexpressed . . . ; no, not unexpressed, because on the red hills of the city stand two palaces, both dead: the Alhambra and the palace of Carlos V, still locked in a duel to the death that beats in the consciousness of every true Granadan.

The traveler who visits Granada must see all this, a Granada, as now, wearing the lush attire of spring. For the big crowds of rowdy tourists, fans of cabarets and grand hotels, those frivolous groups that the people of the Albaicín district dub "those touristy people," the soul of the city will be forever closed.

Translated by Barbara Paschke

Children Can Wait

Nivaria Tejera

I

THE WAR STARTED today. Maybe it's been many days. I don't really understand *when* things start. Suddenly they're happening around me, and people are here I knew from before. I'm not very good at thinking, so for me the war started today opposite Grandpa's house.

That was hours ago. It feels like somewhere in between. I got years older all at once. I look at things the way you do when you miss them. It seems they're not here. "This is the patio of a house. On this patio there's a medlar tree and a big clay jar of water; then a black goat. House, jar, patio, black goat, tree. If someone covers my eyes, I can point to those things without getting any wrong: tree, black goat, patio, jar, house." But it's as if they'd erased my memory and

NIVARIA TEJERA *(1933–) is the daughter of a Cuban mother and a Spanish father who was imprisoned during the War. A poet and novelist, her most recent novel is* Espero la noche para soñarte, Revolución. *She lives in Paris.* The Ravine *(El barranco, 1958), from which this excerpt is taken, is narrated by an unnamed child from the Canary Islands during the civil war. Her father, a Republican, is taken prisoner the first day of the conflict.*

left me lost, far, far away. I keep hearing one word: *war-warwar*. That word seems to be hammering. (Other words break apart, don't exist anymore.) You can't place war, but I feel like it's watching on all sides, another body moving about inside me. The war. Suddenly it's something that's known me for a long time. A long dark corridor where little by little Papa stops smiling.

We were getting ready for the fiesta of Cristo de La Laguna. La Laguna's the town where we live. Auntie had almost finished putting my linen dress on me, the one I was wearing for the first time. She couldn't get the bow tied right. "You're nervous, Auntie," I said, turning around, and she shook her head. I looked through the small glass shutter. "There's something funny going on today," I thought, seeing her face in the shutter. Auntie's a little old. I love her so much I think she should be my mother. She's nice and she doesn't have any children. Auntie makes men's underwear for a clothing store. They don't pay her very much, but she helps Grampy, who makes packsaddles. When she's paid extra, I get toys and the usual dresses. (I don't think this will happen any more. Don't know. I feel sad and confused.) At night, while everyone's asleep, the sound of Auntie's sewing machine travels all the way across the street to my house, like a locomotive that stops in lots of villages. Sometimes I don't close my eyes until her room gets dark. (I think the white threads turning up in her hair these days fall from the lamp during the night.) "That's your dream, Auntie," I said as if remembering out loud. "Which one?" she answered, surprised. "Sewing," I said, and she answered

"Yes," staring at me for a long time. Her eyes welled up and she looked beautiful. I gave her a hug: "Thank you, because if you didn't dream I wouldn't have dresses." She trembled and I understood. Maybe she heard the war before I did, because she's older and thinking is like having a presentiment of things. Of course I was dying to look at myself in the mirror. Papa would be home soon and I could hardly wait for him to see me. He's happy when I wear a new dress. Opens his arms carefully, kneels, and smiles at me: "Where's my ugly little lady?" he says. I run to stand on his thighs and he hugs me until I can't breathe. Then he stands back and spins me round and round so my skirt billows out. As I circle past I see him getting a kiss ready and he starts to sparkle. Mama says I'm his girlfriend, but she says that because she's jealous. She would not be able to understand that, for me, Papa's an enchanted city. Today when he comes back . . . "Auntie, if you don't hurry up, Papa . . ."

That's when the bow Auntie was about to tie crashed against her scream. From deep inside the scream I saw Mama appear with Chicho and Grandpa behind. "The war, it's the war," she was screaming. The noise was bringing the street closer to us. Bolts were banged shut. Trucks, shots, shouts flew back and forth. Dreadful blows made the glass rattle in the doors and the shutter where Auntie's reflection was before. You could tell people were upset. They seemed to be carrying those hoes Grandpa uses to break up the ground at El Barbado when he digs up potatoes. Everyone was racing around so much the corners were coming loose. The wood on the walls was creaking and colliding with the floorboards. We were all part of the same tremor. "They want to get in," I said, touching Mama's arm. "Mama." She paid no attention. Hugging my brother, like always. "Auntie, Grandpa, they want to get in." Neither of them heard. I was scared. "I want to hide," I said. I felt jealous of Chicho and held out my arms to Grampy. But they were busy pushing furniture against the doors so those people couldn't get in. My ears started to ache. I looked for Ñeca on the shelf, hugged her the way Papa hugs me, and crawled under the bed. Tried to think: "The war's made of so much noise; if the shots keep up, my ears will burst." But the only thing I knew was that I felt very alone. Pressed Ñeca against my chest so she couldn't hear, and she said "Aaaaaaaaa," as if it all made her ache.

I was crying and there was a lot of confusion, but I heard Grampy calling me so he could hide me in the room at the end of the patio, before you get to the one with the goats and the chicken coop. Behind us, the house was about to cave in from the blows. Screams slid over the roofs from the street to the patio. Soon, when those people moved on, the street would swallow us up. I felt panicky when I thought of the huge throat that was making that noise. "Here it won't be so dangerous," Mama said. Her green eyes had turned red. Auntie was talking fast, as if to herself. "This was bound to happen. They know Santiago's a Republican. They'll kill us. If we'd only known. Why didn't anyone warn us? How were we to know? And to think that Santiago's not even here. None of you say a word. If only there were someone here, a man I mean. Juan! Juan!" She was calling next door, to Uncle's house. "Oh my God, such awful things; to think we didn't know," she said, and she looked nervous and ugly. I felt sorry for her, and I spoke to her lovingly: "Auntie." Uncle answered from the other patio. "Quiet. This will all be over soon, don't talk anymore." Mama was still trembling. "They'll do us in." Nearby, the goats were chewing their cuds. We could tell it was the goats because the sound they made was different from the other noises. "Ma-ma-ma," Chicho repeated tirelessly. It's almost a word and he wants to be understood. Grampy took me on his lap. He didn't say anything until I asked him: "What about Papa?" Without him I'm always alone.

I thought about the street. To me it looked like a long dagger. At the end, a blurred shape faded into nothing. When I go out to play and they tell me I'm not allowed to go past the corner, I always imagine that the world ends where the street does—that the last curve, the last tree, are the entrance to heaven. Is there a world only as far as I can see? Yes, Papa said. And doesn't the war come from behind the world, from outside it? Yes. But when Papa's driving and the road continues, when we stop to look at the sea or climb the mountain to have a picnic, the world continues. Then it's always a road that never ends. Now I was seeing Papa way in the distance, at the end of that road, at the end of the world, fading into nothing.

I felt so afraid I wouldn't get there in time to save him that my whole body ached. Thought about the birds and wanted to be one of them in order to reach Papa. Looked for Grampy's eyes so I could ask him again. "Papa's at the newspaper, niña," he said. "But those men are coming to get him, aren't they?" I felt his knees stiffen under my behind.

I imagined the street again. Now it was becoming a dark hollow that stretched on and on until it dwindled away. Then, from deep inside me, which was now the deepest part of the hollow, Papa was walking and his body was made of linen. I tried to run to him and hug him, to warn him not to come. But I felt my linen dress pressing against me. And the linen-Papa was me hugging myself because I was afraid. I touched my dress and now it had no shape, was a dead dress. Mama and Chicho seemed to be one trembling person. Grandpa's knees got pointy, like two thorns. I stroked my dress harder, imagined I was touching Papa's body, wherever he was. Auntie was twisting my curls, and her fear was coming through them. I felt much better because between her and Grandpa someone was taking care of me. But "What about Papa?" Grandpa shivered, and then he rocked me like he does when he wants me to fall asleep. "Be quiet, niña," he said, "he'll be here soon." His voice got drier: "You'll see, he'll be here soon." I thought it was a lie. (He's worried because he suspects I don't believe him.) I smiled to fool him. Grandpa's eyes clouded over and he pressed his lips to my head. The top of my skull felt warm because of his breathing. He sat that way for a long time.

From the street came a rush of words: "Drop your weapons, hands up, open the door or we'll knock it down, up with the Right, down with the Left, death to them, death." They kept saying the same thing over and over as if they didn't know how to say anything else. I noticed that my heart was getting smaller or that they were locking it up with lots of keys. "Go to sleep, niña," Grandpa urged, squeezing me tight against his chest.

"Niña, niña, niña, niñaaaaaaa." Another familiar voice. I fell into it like falling into emptiness. Crying. Underneath, Papa smiled, sparkling as if it were morning. Now I could not tell where the noise was coming from. Walls shaking, painful jabs in my ears, terrible cold freezing my forehead, the wrinkles in grandpa's neck jumping over my face like ants. I cried harder. Tried to get free. "Papa, paaaa," I shouted. Forgot all the people, the street. I had to find him, because something was getting hard, something that's always soft inside, that Grandpa's hands release when he plunges the sewing needles through the packsaddle leather, that I can't see although it scratches my skin when Papa kisses me. I fell and managed to crawl to the patio. But suddenly a crash pushed the house toward us, like someone falling on his back. I stopped. What was it? The war? While those men came closer, the wood in the house moaned as if they were hurting it. I felt sorry for the house because it couldn't run away, for Chicho, who kept saying "ma-ma-ma-ma-ma," and for Grandpa, who was old.

They were all talking at once. I could hear isolated words: "Your weapons, the Right, the general, the Left, up with, down with, long live, death to, damn them, up with him, down with them, scoundrel, fox, bastard, dog, flag, rape, morals, road, the whole street, that way, patria, this way, shots, search, search, search, national uprising, long live the general, there's no light, prison, search wherever they are, search, search." Several of them appeared. They wore dark caps and gray uniforms. Rifles hung from their shoulders. I looked at Mama, who was pulling at my curls. Squeezed Grandpa's sleeve with one hand. "They're the *arribistas*," he said when he saw them. With the other hand I pinched Auntie's fat arm. "They're the *arribistas*," she answered. They said things I couldn't hear or understand. "Where's he hiding?" one of them screamed. "Who?" Grandpa asked. "The little boy," someone else said. (I looked at Chicho sucking on his dummy, his eyes opened wide); Grandpa stared right at them. "Are you talking about my son?" One of them who wore shields with flags painted on them and ships on his sleeves replied that this was no joking matter and called to some others. "Where's the man of the house, you old sot?" they demanded, shaking him and kicking over two pots of ferns while they talked. "I am," Grandpa answered. I looked at him. "He's Grandpa," I said, and they all laughed. One ordered the others to search the shed and the platform where he keeps the straw. Some of them I recognized because they used to visit Papa on Sundays, and I could see from the middle of the patio how they were turning the shed upside down. (Grandpa sits there as soon as it's light, making packsaddles for people who come from the country, which means they're all very poor and have donkeys or horses or carts, because they're peasants who live far away near El Barbado, where the mountains make it impossible to see the sky. No one in La Laguna knows how to measure the back of a mule like Grandpa. The mules smile at him when he's finished, prancing around as if they were going to eat him up, because that's how they show their thanks to him for understanding them. Grandpa pulls at their ears, their snouts, their hides, and I've even seen him take off their ticks and then tend the wounds. And when one-eyed *chó* Pedro el Tuerto or *seña* Encarnación Perejila, whose name sounds like the Spanish word for parsley, ride up the path on their mules, he rubs his hands together happily, as if relieved of a great burden. Then he goes inside and starts to work on the packsaddle he was making before. Sometimes I hide in there to scare him. Grandpa's nice and he doesn't talk much. Some days he says things that make me laugh, but he never lifts his eyes from what he's doing. He has a paddle he uses to spank me on the behind if I'm bad, but at night, when he eats his oatmeal from the big cup, he makes a hollow on his lap and lets me sit there so I can blow on the oatmeal and cool it off for him. Then he plays a lullaby on his guitar so I'll fall asleep, sings *coplas* in a soft voice, and rocks me gently. I don't go to sleep right away, and then he tells me about something that once happened to him long ago. Auntie says we often fall asleep together. "You're the same age," she says, "two children." He *is* just like a friend. But to me he never stops being Grandpa.)

I remembered as I watched the men search his shed. They came back across the straw, bringing Yolí and holding him up in the air by his fur. "Yolí," I shouted, and he tried to sneak away. "Yolí," I said again, and he ran over to lick me. We hugged each other. I thought of Papa. "Where is he?" I asked the tallest man. Now I wasn't afraid. They were looking behind the wardrobes, under the beds, searching Grandpa's trunks and making a lot of noise. Outside, trucks and shouts seemed to shatter the street. "Who?" they asked. For some reason, Papa began to appear in that group of gray figures, as if he were one of them. "Where's Papa?" I murmured, crossing Yolí's paws around my neck and looking at Mama and Chicho who were still trembling. I went up to the tall one. "Hey, where is he?" The man pushed me to one side, and I saw the dark street again. Auntie and Mama were crying. Mama was saying "My husband" and Auntie was saying "my dear brother." "For the last time," the man shouted next to Grandpa, "where is your son, you old brute? There's a warrant out for his arrest." He shook him. "Answer." But Grandpa lowered his eyes. He looked more stooped from where I was watching and he seemed even farther away. I saw that the man was shaking Grandpa and I wanted to hug him. I felt that I loved him more than Papa because he was there and he'd wilted. I placed myself between the two of them. "He doesn't know," I said, letting go of Yolí, "but I do. He's at the end of the street." I looked at the others. "Today there is no street, niña," one of them explained. The racket continued. Suddenly I hated Papa for not being with us, for not looking after me or defending poor Grandpa. More men arrived; they said something in secret and left together. One of them pulled my curls. Auntie got nervous: "Now they know where he is, what will they do?" and she ran after them; Mama followed her, complaining silently to herself, so she could hear their answer.

Grandpa walked toward the shed. It was dark because there's no lamp. In one corner Yolí's always tied at the foot of the cistern and in the other corner Uncle puts the bus tires he collects; on some planks near the ceiling where it's damp are the packsaddles with rotten leather that Grandpa will fix so he can sell them as good as new. "Life," I heard him say as he walked, and I sensed that life, whatever it was, even if I didn't know, was moving in the same direction as Grandpa: toward the shed, the dampness, the cistern, Yolí tied by his foot, all that deflated rubber ("today there is no street"; now it will always be today, I won't forget this day), and the rotten packsaddles too, "worn out for the road, ready for sausage," like in Grandpa's song.

I glanced down toward the far end of the platform where the clear yellow straw makes me think of light, moving. Grandpa was a shape that looked like another corner of the platform in the middle of the straw shop. I went over to the medlar tree. Wished I could have reached a medlar and opened it. Medlars are the same color as straw, and they're soft. "Grandpa." I heard him sobbing. Maybe he was dying. "Death to them, death to them," those people were saying.

"Niña." Grandpa was calling. I walked through the shed without realizing it. "Listen," he began, "Papa will be on another island for a long time." "Why?" I asked. "Politics," Grandpa said. He tried to explain this to me quickly. "Imagine a sidewalk with a different camp on each side. Since the two are separated, see, they're enemies. Papa is on this side, and he lost." I didn't understand very well, but I searched for his eyes. "What did he lose?" Grandpa thought for a moment. "Well, freedom, you, me. He won't be able to see us." I thought about where he would go then. We could go if we knew where he was, or I could go, even if neither Mama nor Grandpa nor Auntie wanted to. I remembered what the men in uniform had said: "morals . . . patria . . . rape." (Which one would be the place?) Grandpa moved his eyes close to my curls, as if he were looking for a handkerchief. (He's going to cry.) His hand was hard and it felt heavy as it brushed my forehead, heavier than when he wanted me to fall asleep. "Grandpa, what's in your hand?" I asked. "A fixed thought," he answered, but I didn't understand. His voice was dry again. Like when he has heartburn. I was sitting on his knees, watching how the little bits of straw crisscrossed playfully on the floor. "Papa will go to an island called jail," he said. Out there the street continued: voices, shots, distance. Jail, jail, I thought, and I said, "What's that? Grandpa, what is that?" I asked, raising my head. I lifted his face by the chin so I could look into his eyes: "What is that?" "We'll find out later," he answered harshly.

Auntie and Mama came. They were still crying and that made them seem funny. My brother had stopped repeating "ma-ma-ma"; he was crying too, lying on Mama's shoulder, and he seemed to understand the danger. He'd bitten through his dummy and there was a hole in it.

Now I don't want to hear any more. Behind me a whole lot of sentences are breaking nice ugly Auntie in two—Auntie who said "my dear brother" when she talked about Papa. But I escape to the patio. Auntie's something way out there, the street. Like a wall collapsing violently. Mama's fading away as well. It's like one mute tormenting another. There are no screams in her kind of suffering, and that makes her more tiresome. She and Auntie are on good terms now, although they never got along well. Grandpa, who's more alone, is a "sowing" plagued by droughts—he calls his vegetable garden a sowing. "Droughts aren't germs, but they sure make you sick," he says. Even Auntie speaks her mind sometimes, but not so often, not so often. The floor seems to be falling in too. I need to think. But something's pushing me, and I feel weak. An invisible hand's spinning me round and round. My dress swirls, billows out. I keep looking: tree, jar, platform and straw, black goat. Everything's swirling in circles, like when Papa . . .

The word "prisoner" comes from prison island. I'll look in the dictionary: "He's being held prisoner." Prison from from . . . I don't know. "We'll find out later, jail, we'll find out later, a fixed thought, we'll find out later." Grandpa. That meant, "Jail is a fixed thought." I go back to the shed. "Listen, Grandpa, jail is . . ."

Won't ask any more questions. All four of them are over there, staring at the floor. Hard to see them very well now that it's getting dark. They seem like little shadows playing together. I'll go pick up the ferns, their dirt's fallen out. Those men kicked them. I run to the kitchen. "Mules," I'll shout at them, Grandpa will make them some packsaddles, "mules." But no, they're gone now, everything's quiet. It seems as though there's no kitchen left. My ferns, broken, covered with some bitter green liquid. "Mules, mules." Poor Papa. I think how one day they'll beat him the way they did the ferns; Papa's heart will be green like that and release the same acid juice when they hurt him, and there won't be any hands to pick him up.

But, what did Papa do? Today was the fiesta. He should have come home early. He likes to walk under the candles they light when the procession comes out of the tower at midnight and there are two rows of people all the way to the plaza at the foot of the mountain. Then the city belongs to us like at no other time. Besides, now there's no fiesta.

I hear Auntie's voice. "They've declared war. They'll spill blood among themselves, all of them sons of the same patria . . ." (morals . . . patria . . . rape) I cover my ears, don't want to listen any more.

Waaarwaaarwaaar. That word will shatter me. I'm afraid and it's standing guard; I'm cold and it's standing guard. And Papa out there disappearing. "Where can he be?" Now's when I really miss him. He was coming back from the newspaper, smiling. No, today I won't see him, he's hidden in the war. In the house, Grandpa and everyone calling him in secret, but he doesn't hear. He's walking beneath that uproar, in the street.

And now I won't grow. I feel as if I've already grown up. A war can arrest children. Even though children don't fight and don't go to prison and last longer.

Children can wait.

11

When I woke up this morning it was Sunday.

I found out because Grandpa came into Auntie's room and he was wearing his suit with a waistcoat. I've been sleeping here since "the coup," because it's where they came to search for Papa and this way I can feel close to him. I heard Grandpa shaking Auntie in bed. She complained, slurring her words drowsily. "Listen, *jija*," he said, as if asking permission from his own daughter and saying that word his way, not saying *hija:* "I'm going to city hall to ask don Pancho for advice." I felt a chill. The other afternoon when Mama was talking with Uncle, she told him: "I think don Pancho's from the 'movement.'" I lifted one edge of the sheet. Auntie put her finger to her mouth, forcing me to be quiet and looked at me out of the corner of her eye. She knows I listen to everything. Grandpa came closer. He obeys Auntie, as if she were his mother. "*Jija*, the *pelotón*'s still going on and I'm nervous. The rheumatism in my joints is so bad I can't work. Remember that I'm old," he added. Auntie shook him affectionately by the lapels. "All right, Pa, hold up that head." Then she helped him stand straight. "And take good care of yourself, mind you." He went off and I realized that his suit is seasick, because he sways wearily from side to side. Yes, Grandpa does seem older. He reminded me of one of his worn-out saddlepacks. My eyes half-open, I could see that Auntie was tiptoeing toward the door of the room, wrapped in a blanket. "Listen, Pa, tell him the girl cries every day, ask him to do everything he possibly can." And she walked slowly back to bed. His footsteps went down to the street and all you could see of him through the windowpane was his hat, as if it were Grandpa. Auntie sighed, looking toward the wall in front of her. "If don Pancho . . ." She pulled the covers over herself again and turned over in bed; I hugged the pillow and pretended to snore.

Don Pancho is Chicho's godfather and he always gives Chicho money, which they keep for him in a tin bank for when he grows up. Besides, don Pancho's the mayor of La Laguna and it's important to know him. He walks with crutches, and when Chicho goes to visit him, don Pancho sits him on top of one crutch and rocks him back and forth. Don Pancho annoys me because he's very nosy. Is Chicho going to talk, is he good, have his green eyes gotten bigger, do I study a lot, are we going to the movies (he gives us money to go), is the dog our friend . . . He finds this amusing. I like his house; it's big and dark, and easy to get lost in. If I lived there, he'd never notice I was home and this would make me happy (it's awful that everybody knows what you're doing). Sometimes I walk through the house and it makes me imagine a magical country inside the flowerpots with their gigantic plants that shade the fountain, or I follow the passageway that runs around the patio. All those climbing plants make a noise, since they grow as high as the wooden railing in the upstairs hallway and they creak in chorus when it's very windy. The walls (or something behind them) seem to be moving, as if they were breathing or felt cold. The house is behind the church. Even that far away you can hear the organ music and the silence so well you imagine you're right on the roof of the chapel. I don't think time moves from one hour to the next there like it does on all the other clocks. Besides, when the bells ring, lots of little birds all wake up together and swirl round and round the way my linen dress did before. Then while they perch on the railings on the patio at night, their music mimics the bells for a long time. Since the house can't compete with so much shade, it vanishes. The last day we were there, Auntie, who's very religious, took me to church. We've gone four times this week. "Pray and then ask for Papa to come back," she tells me. But I look at those stone or cardboard figures nailed to the wall and I don't see God. My mind wanders and Auntie keeps repeating, "Look for him, look for him," as if God were a ball lost behind some door. Then I think since God's so large and powerful he'll let us see him if he's really there, and I sit still to see if he'll come. I can't imagine God the way he's painted in those pictures, with a body like Grandpa's, going to the toilet, blowing his nose, or being sleepy. I don't believe that God has a size; he's the air; like one afternoon when we went up into the mountains and the world stayed below, or like Yolí's eyes, which smile and don't ask for anything, or like the pigeons when they disappear in the sky. But on those dirty broken church benches where my knees get scratched, if Auntie pinches me ("pray so I can hear you"), I fold my hands and start to say "againagainagainagain" out loud, as if I were praying. Makes me start muttering as soon as I think about leaving there.

It's been three weeks now of looking for Papa without finding out anything. We walked through enormous buildings that seemed like palaces and are called court houses. At the entrance there are some small glass windows where they put lists filled with names that tell who was in the last *pelotón*. That's how they let people know who's not alive any longer. No one talks in front of me, and when they take me along on those agonizing walks (because I cry so they'll let me go with them), the ones where you get tired since there's no fixed direction, they sit me on one of the long benches where people wait for news. One of the guards entertains me, or maybe Auntie points out some other children going by and how the sun is gilding the little plazas. But when we get home I listen behind the doors to what they're saying. Now I know that what they call a *pelotón* is a group of men they take away to kill in the Tanqueabajo, an enormous ravine all overgrown with weeds, where they throw dead animals and garbage from the city. Then they leave them there and let them rot and their families don't find out because they trick them by saying they're in prison. And when the families try to find out more they tell them they're still under arrest. Month after month like that. It's horrible to find this out and afterward I can't forget it. If only I had someone to tell about this so that person would suffer too and would not forget either. But no one's interested.

Translated by Carol Maier

PETER BUSH (1946–) is Director of the Sebald International Centre for Literary Translation at the University of East Anglia. He edited *The Voice of the Turtle*, an anthology of Cuban stories (Grove), and has translated work by Nuria Amat, Juan Goytisolo, Juan Carlos Onetti, Orlando González Esteva, Senel Paz, and Luis Sepúlveda, among others. His translation of Goytisolo's *The Marx Family Saga* won the Valle-Inclán Prize and his translation of Luis Sepúlveda's *The Old Man Who Read Love Stories*, a Best Translation of the Year Award from the American Literary Translator's Association.

LISA DILLMAN (1967–) has translated Spanish, Catalan, Cuban, and Argentinian fiction, including the novel *Pot Pourri: Whistlings of a Vagabond* by Eugenio Cambaceres (Oxford University Press, 2003). Her most recent projects include a collection of Argentinian poetry, as well as the testimonies of Cuban, Chilean, and Guatamalan women revolutionaries. She teaches translation and Spanish in the Spanish department at Emory University.

MARGARET JULL COSTA has translated many novels and short stories by Portuguese, Spanish, and Latin American writers, among them Mário de Sá-Carneiro, José Régio, Bernardo Atxaga, Carmen Martín Gaite, Ramón del Valle-Inclán, Rafael Sánchez Ferlosio, Juan José Saer, and Luis Fernando Verissimo. She has won numerous prizes for her translations, including the Weidenfeld Translation Prize for

José Saramago's *All the Names*. At the time of this publication, she is preparing new translations of all the novels of Eça de Queiroz for Dedalus Books.

D.A. DÉMERS is a translator, literary critic, and associate editor of *Caliban*. She lives in Madrid.

COLA FRANZEN lives in Cambridge, Massachusetts, and translates the creative work of Alicia Borinsky, Saúl Yurkievich, and Juan Cameron. She has also translated works by Claudio Guillén and Guillermo Núñez. She is a member and past secretary-treasurer of ALTA (American Literary Translators Association) and vice-president of Language Research, Inc. in Cambridge, Massachusetts.

AMAIA GABANTXO was born in the Basque country, where she grew up speaking both Basque and Spanish. She moved to England at age 20, and began to write in English. She now lives in Norwich, teaching literature at the University of East Anglia and writing reviews for the *Times Literary Supplement*.

HELEN LANE has translated the work of Juan Goytisolo, Octavio Paz, Luisa Valenzuela, Juan José Saer, Ernesto Sábato, and Mario Vargas Llosa, and has received many awards—notably the NBA, the Gulbenkian, and PEN Club Translation Prizes. She lives in Albuquerque, New Mexico.

CAROL MAIER teaches Spanish and translation at Kent State University (USA), where she serves as graduate coordinator and is affiliated with the Institute for Applied Linguistics. Her translations include Rosa Chacel's *Memoirs of Leticia Valle*, María Zambrano's *Delirium and Destiny*, Octavio Armand's *Refractions*, and (with Suzanne Jill Levine) Severo Sarduy's *Christ on the Rue Jacob*. Her essay about the poetics of exile appears in *Translation and Power,* edited by Maria Tymozcko and Edwin Gentzler.

JOHN MCCARTHY is a translator and interpreter based in London who also lectures on translation and interpreting at a number of universities. In addition to literary and academic projects he also works in legal and social aid for refugees, commercial translation, and conference interpreting.

ANNE MCLEAN studied history in London, Ontario, and literary translation in London, England. She has translated Latin American and Spanish novels, short stories, memoirs, and other writings by authors including Julio Cortázar, Orlando González Esteva, Ignacio Padilla, Luis Sepúlveda, and Paula Varsavsky. Her most recent translations are *Living's the Strange Thing* by Carmen Martín Gaite and *Soldiers of Salamis* by Javier Cercas.

BARBARA PASCHKE is a freelance translator who lives in San Francisco. Her publications include *Riverbed of Memory* (City Lights), translations of poems by Daisy Zamora of Nicaragua, and a children's story by Alberto Blanco from Mexico (*The Desert Mermaid,* Children's Book Press). She has co-edited two books of Central American poetry in translation (*Volcan,* City Lights Books, and *Clandestine Poems,* Curbstone) and one of Central American short stories (*Clamor of Innocence,* City Lights). She has contributed translations to a number of books, including *Tomorrow Triumphant* (selected poems of Otto Rene Castillo, Night Horn Books), two volumes of short stories from Whereabouts Press (*Costa Rica* and *Cuba*), and numerous journals.

BARBARA D. RIESS, assistant professor of Spanish at Allegheny College, received her Ph.D. in Latin American Literature and Translation from Arizona State University in

1999. Co-translator of the underground classic Chicano novel *Puppet* (New Mexico Press, 2001), with articles published in journals and encyclopedias, her most recent project is a collection of stories by Cuban author María Elena Llana: *Havana's Ghosts: Those That Neither Left Nor Stayed Behind.*

JOHN RUTHERFORD is a fellow of The Queen's College, Oxford, where he teaches Spanish, Spanish-American, and Galician language and literature. He has also translated *La Regenta* by Leopoldo Alas (Clarín) and *Don Quixote* by Miguel de Cervantes Saavedra, both for Penguin Classics. At Oxford he runs a weekly Galician Translation Workshop, the members of which helped with the translation from the Galician language of the story by Méndez Ferrín. For the translation of *La Regenta* he was decorated in 1984 by King Juan Carlos of Spain with the Medalla de Oro al Mérito en las Bellas Artes.

CRISTINA DE LA TORRE has translated three novels: *Absent Love (Crónica del desamor)* by Rosa Montero (Spain), *Mirror Images (Joc de miralls/Por persona interpuesta)* by Carme Riera (Spain), and *A Single, Numberless Death (Una sola muerte numerosa)* by Nora Strejilevich (Argentina) as well as numerous short stories. She lives in Atlanta and teaches Spanish at Emory University.

English as *The Fallen* and in Spanish as *Si te dicen que caí.* © 1973 by Juan Marsé. English translation © 1979, 1994 (revised) by Helen Lane. Published by permission of the author.

Xosé Luís Méndez Ferrín's "Sibila" was published in *Them and Other Stories* (1996). © 1996 by Xosé Luís Méndez Ferrín. English translation © 1996 by John Rutherford. Translated and published by permission of the author.

Quim Monzó's "The Five Doorstops" was originally published in *El millor dels mons* © 2001 by Quim Monzó; © 2001 by Quaderns Crema, S.A. English translation © 2003 by Peter Bush. Translated and published by permission of Quaderns Crema, S.A.

Javier Puebla's "Mamá" was originally published in *Lavapiés* © 2001 by Javier Puebla. English translation © 2003 by Cola Franzen. Translated and published by permission of the author.

Fernando Quiñones's "Right All Along" was originally published as "Siempre tuvimos razón" in *Cinco historias del vino* © 1969 by Fernando Quiñones. English translation © 2003 by Cristina de la Torre. Published by permission of Nadia Consolani.

Carme Riera's "Is Angela There?" was originally published in *Te deix, amor, la mar, com a penyora* in 1975 © by Carme Riera. English translation © 2003 by Lisa Dillman. Translated and published by permission of the author.

Manuel Rivas's "The Confession" was originally published as "A confesión" in *As chamadas perdidas* © 2001 by Manuel Rivas. English translation © 2003 by Margaret Jull Costa. Translated and published by permission of La Oficina del Autor.

Germán Sierra's "Amnesia" © 2003 by Germán Sierra was first published in *El Extramundi* magazine in 1997. English translation © 2003 by Lisa Dillman. Translated and published by permission of the author.

Nivaria Tejera's "Children Can Wait" is excerpted from the novel *El barranco (The Ravine)* © 1958 by Nivaria Tejera. English translation © 2003 by Carol Maier. Translated and published by permission of the author.

Angela Vallvey's "Sex, Food, and the Family" is an excerpt from *Hunting the Last Wild Man.* English translation © 2002 by Margaret Jull Costa. First published in Spain as *A la caza del último hombre salvaje* by Emecé Editores © 1999 by Angela Vallvey. Published by permission of Penguin Books in the UK and Seven Story Press in the US.